The Well-Being of Canada

Le bien-être du Canada

The Well-Being of Canada

Proceedings of a symposium held in November 1997 under the
auspices of the Royal Society of Canada

Le bien-être du Canada

Actes d'un colloque tenu en novembre 1997 sous les auspices de la
Société royale du Canada

Organized by / Organisé par

T. Geoffrey Flynn, FRSC, President, Academy of Science
Président, Académie des sciences

Edited by / sous la direction de

David M. Hayne, FRSC

Transactions of the Royal Society of Canada, Series VI, Volume VIII, 1997
Mémoires de la Société royale du Canada, Sixième série, Tome VIII, 1997

Published for the Royal Society of Canada by
University of Toronto Press

Toronto   Buffalo   London

University of Toronto Press acknowledges the assistance to its publishing program of the Canada Council and the Ontario Arts Council.

National Library of Canada cataloguing

Royal Society of Canada
    Transactions of the Royal Society of Canada =
Mémoires de la Société royale du Canada

Annual.
1882-
Text in English and French.
ISSN 0035-9122
ISBN 0-8020-8256-4 (vol. VIII, sixth series)

    1. Science—Canada—Collected Works. I. Title.
II. Title: Mémoires de la Société royale du Canada.

AS42.R66   081   C75-030369-7E

Catalogage de la Bibliothèque nationale du Canada

Société royale du Canada
    Transactions of the Royal Society of Canada =
Mémoires de la Société royale du Canada

Annuel.   .
1882-
Texte en anglais et en français.
ISSN 0035-9122
ISBN 0-8020-8256-4 (tome VIII, sixième série)

    1. Sciences—Canada—Collections. I. Titre.
II. Titre: Mémoires de la Société royale du Canada.

AS42.R66   081   C75-030369-7F

Contents / Matières

Two contributions to the program of the Symposium are not included in this volume: Professor Aritha van Herk's luncheon address "Warm Heart, Weak Pulse: The Culture Condition" has appeared in the January-February 1998 issue of *The Canadian Forum*. Mr. Jay Ingram's informal talk "Communicating Science to Canadians" may be consulted on audio tape by arrangement with the Society's Secretariat.

Deux des contributions au programme du Colloque ne sont pas reprises dans ce volume : la causerie prononcée par la professeure Aritha van Herk pendant le déjeuner sous le titre « Warm Heart, Weak Pulse: The Culture Condition » a été publiée dans le numéro de janvier-février 1998 de la revue *The Canadian Forum* et la causerie à bâtons rompus de Monsieur Jay Ingram sur le thème « Communicating Science to Canadians » est disponible sur bande magnétique auprès du secrétariat de la Société.

T. GEOFFREY FLYNN, FRSC

Introduction

For the past several years, this country has suffered economic and political stress that has taken a significant toll on the collective psyche. Economically, we have been beset by a crippling deficit and debt that has affected our general marketability abroad and restrained development at home. We have seen the rise of a new political party and the virtual demise of another party of the right. The closeness of the vote of the Quebec referendum took us to the brink of partition. It seems somehow fitting, therefore, that we should, at this time, reflect deeply on the state of our nation, particularly as we approach the end of the century and the much vaunted millennium.

The Royal Society of Canada has responded to our past and current situation with two symposia. The first, held in November 1996, was stimulated by the close results of the Quebec referendum of October 1995 and undertook to reflect on the future of Canada and on possible solutions to the problems threatening our very existence as a nation. This symposium was entitled "Can Canada Survive? Under What Terms and Conditions".

The November 1997 symposium of the Royal Society of Canada was in many ways a natural successor to the 1996 symposium. It asked the question—how well are we doing as a nation?—and the symposium was entitled "The Well Being of Canada". Speakers chosen from within and outside the Royal Society of Canada were asked to examine how well Canada is doing in areas that are important for the health and welfare of Canadians. The areas chosen were health and health care, science and technology, culture, education, and the economy. Most of the papers presented at the symposium are collected in this volume. Readers will find that speakers, for the most part, addressed the question—how well are we doing?—openly and honestly and revealed both our weaknesses and strengths in the areas they addressed. Discussion of the papers was wide ranging and incisive, and while those present would not for a moment conclude that definitive solutions were found, clearly the question asked was pertinent and a deeper understanding of the issues presented was achieved.

The planning of a symposium such as this cannot be done by a single individual. I am grateful for the sage advice of the other members of the

T. Geoffrey Flynn

Planning Committee—Robert Haynes, John Woods, Patrice Garant, David Hayne and Pat Smart. I am particularly grateful to Nancy Schenk for her organizing skills and for her timely advice based on her deep knowledge and understanding of the Royal Society of Canada.

Depuis plusieurs années, le Canada est en proie à un stress économique et politique qui a lourdement hypothéqué la psyché collective. Au plan économique, nous avons été obérés par une dette publique et un déficit paralysants qui ont entravé notre compétitivité à l'étranger et limité notre développement intérieur. Nous avons été témoins de la montée en puissance d'un nouveau parti politique et de la disparition virtuelle d'un autre parti de droite. Le résultat serré du référendum au Québec nous a amenés au bord de l'éclatement. Il semble dès lors assez opportun que nous soyons maintenant amenés à nous livrer à une réflexion profonde sur l'état de notre nation, d'autant plus que nous sommes à la veille d'une fin de siècle et à l'aube de ce nouveau millénaire dont on fait tant de cas.

La Société royale du Canada a réagi à notre situation passée et présente par deux colloques. Le premier, qui a eu lieu en novembre 1996, a été suscité par l'issue serrée du référendum tenu au Québec en octobre 1995 et a consisté en une réflexion sur l'avenir du Canada et sur les solutions possibles aux problèmes qui menaçaient notre existence même en tant que nation. Il eut pour thème « Le Canada peut-il encore survivre? Comment et dans quelles conditions ? »

Le colloque de novembre 1997 allait à bien des égards s'inscrire dans le droit fil de celui de 1996. Par son intitulé, « Le bien-être du Canada », il posait en effet comme question « comment nous en tirons-nous en tant que nation? » Des conférenciers, membres ou non de la Société royale, avaient été appelés à analyser la performance relative de notre pays dans des domaines importants pour la santé et le bien-être des Canadiens. Ces domaines étaient la santé et le système médico-hospitalier, les sciences et la technologie, la culture, l'instruction publique et l'économie. La plupart des communications présentées au colloque ont été colligées dans ce volume. Le lecteur y constatera que les conférenciers ont pour l'essentiel répondu avec franchise et sans détours à la question qui leur était posée—comment nous en tirons-nous ?—en révélant à la fois nos points forts et nos faiblesses dans les domaines qu'ils avaient abordés. Les discussions qui entourèrent les communications furent incisives et allèrent tous azimuts mais, bien qu'aucun participant n'ait pu conclure, n'eût été que l'ombre d'un instant, que nous avions ainsi pu découvrir des solutions péremptoires, il demeure évident que la question elle-même était pertinente et qu'il fut ainsi possible d'aboutir à un entendement plus profond de la problématique.

La préparation d'un colloque comme celui-là ne saurait être l'œuvre d'une seule et unique personne. Je suis donc reconnaissant, pour leurs conseils éclairés, aux autres membres du comité de planification, en l'occurrence Robert Haynes, John Woods, Patrice Garant, David Hayne et Pat Smart. Je veux également remercier tout particulièrement Nancy Schenk pour ses talents d'organisatrice et ses conseils à point nommé, fruits de sa connaissance profonde et de sa compréhension de la Société royale du Canada.

DUNCAN G. SINCLAIR

Health Services in Canada—The State We're In

Abstract

Canada's health services system risks being unable to meet the needs of our population into the 21st century. We do not have a single system: we have twelve systems loosely co-ordinated under the Canada Health Act. These provincial and territorial systems are almost exclusively concerned with physicians' services and hospital care; they are not well organized complexes of varied health services, nor are they completely publicly funded. Our so-called health care system is admired elsewhere, yet it has serious weaknesses. There is no correlation between our spending on health care and the actual health of the population. Our growing expenditures on health care have already contributed to a massive public debt and there is no assurance we shall be able to fund the health care needs of our ageing population in the future. We have far more accurate information about the nation's credit card use than about our health care services. Our most urgent need is a nation-wide health information system that will report on the cost-effectiveness of our present practices and the outlays required for the future.

Résumé

Le système des services de santé au Canada risque de ne plus pouvoir répondre aux besoins de la population au 21e siècle. Nous n'avons pas un système unique, nous en avons douze, vaguement coordonnés sous la férule de la Loi canadienne sur la santé. Les régies provinciales et territoriales sont presque exclusivement axées sur les actes médicaux et les services hospitaliers au lieu d'être des systèmes bien orchestrés offrant une variété de services médico-sanitaires. Elles ne sont pas non plus intégralement financées par l'État. Notre prétendu système de soins de santé est admiré à l'étranger, et pourtant il présente de graves lacunes. Il n'existe aucune corrélation entre ce que nous dépensons pour la santé et l'état de santé général de la population. L'accroissement de nos dépenses dans le domaine de la santé a déjà considérablement alourdi la dette publique, et rien ne permet de croire que, dans l'avenir, nous aurons encore les moyens d'assurer les besoins médico-sanitaires de notre population vieillissante. Nous en savons beaucoup plus long sur l'utilisation des cartes de crédit que sur nos services de santé. Ce dont nous avons le plus impérieusement besoin, c'est un système national d'information sur la santé qui nous permette de juger de l'efficacité et de la rentabilité de ce que nous faisons actuellement et des moyens financiers dont nous aurons besoin pour l'avenir.

I am grateful to Dr. Flynn for this opportunity to speak to the Royal Society of Canada on my perception of the state of Canada's health services system. It is a pleasure to share the platform with my distinguished colleague, Henry Friesen, who will speak about the state of Canada's research system. As I will point out, the two are related.

Briefly, I believe Canada's health services system is at risk of not being able to meet the needs of our population into the 21st century. We have insufficient knowledge derived from research either to predict those needs accurately or to know how best to organize the so-called system and ourselves to meet them and pay for their provision. I am looking forward to Dr. Friesen's assessment of the capacity of the research "system" to generate that knowledge and diminish the risk of our not being able to pass on to our successors better tools for health than we enjoy.

Canada does not have a single health services system. We have twelve—ten provincial and two territorial—"systems" loosely co-ordinated with one another by virtue of the fact that their basic characteristics qualify under the Canada Health Act for just enough federal funding to make "staying in line" worthwhile. Stronger glue, however, rests with the citizenry of each province and territory who clearly want "Medicare" to work as if it were a national program.

"Medicare," shorthand for our publicly-funded health services system, is Canada's most cherished social program. Poll after poll confirms that it has become a defining characteristic of what it means to be Canadian. Most of us believe and are proud that this country has among the best, if not **the** best social service program in the developed world to provide our citizens with health and health care services.

Tommy Douglas and his fellow pioneering CCF collectivists in Saskatchewan introduced hospital insurance in 1946 and medical insurance in 1962. Bribed by the federal government with two-for-one dollars and envious of Saskatchewan's lead, all provinces introduced universal, tax-supported hospital and later medical insurance as their first significant post-war steps toward collectivism. By collectivism I mean the commitment of society to share the risk of disease that was previously borne alone by those affected, their families, and others who would extend them charity.

I hasten to add that this commitment to sharing publicly the risk of disease and injury is far from complete. Of the $75 billion spent on health care in Canada annually, 72 percent is "shared" from the public purse. More than a quarter (28 percent) is paid for by individuals, either directly by reaching in their pockets for the money to pay for prescriptions, chiropractic or rehabilitation services, co-payments in nursing homes, etc., or by paying premiums to private insurance carriers. We have **partial** publicly-funded health care in Canada.

The primary purpose of any nation's health services system (some would argue the overarching purpose of the nation as a whole[1]) is to optimize the health and well-being of its population.

But if you rank-ordered all the determinants necessary for an individual to optimize his or her health, many would come before health care services. One of the most profound contributors to good health is a protected, nurturing, secure, stimulating childhood in the midst of a loving family and supportive community. Lifestyle is also important—don't smoke! Clean water, sanitation services, and other public health measures we in Canada take for granted are major contributors. Well educated people live longer in good health than those less well educated. Good housing, good nutrition, the security of steady employment, and the challenge of having useful work to do are all major determinants of health. Being confidently in charge of your own destiny is also very important; those who direct businesses live longer in good health than their middle managers who, in turn, are healthier than production workers.

The state of Canada's health services so-called "system" is that it exhibits very few of the characteristics of a genuine system; and it is lopsided.

A system is defined[2] as "a complex whole; a set of connected things or parts; an organized body of material or immaterial things." Our twelve loosely coordinated "systems" of health care do not constitute a "whole set of connected parts." The sledgehammers of Regional Health Authorities and Ontario's Health Services Restructuring Commission are only now beginning to affect the walls around autonomous hospitals, the so-called "stovepipes" within the "silo" of hospital services. Hospitals compete. They don't work well together and even less well with home care, long-term care, and the many other categories of care that must work together in a genuine health services system, including the care provided by physicians, be it primary, secondary, tertiary, or quaternary care, the latter the newest term for ultra-specialized procedures. And hospitals are only one of the many prominent "silos" in health and health care.

As for lopsided, Canada's "Medicare" deals almost exclusively with health care or sickness care, as it is referred to straightforwardly in Sweden.[3] In fact, "Medicare" deals primarily with sickness as it is treated by physicians and in hospitals. As important as hospital and physicians' services are, there are many other services necessary in the spectrum to provide health care. And health care services, relatively speaking, contribute far less to health than many other factors that receive less public attention and far less political and financial support.

However non-systematic and lopsided it may be, Canada's health care system gets high marks both internally and internationally.

The National Forum on Health opined earlier this year that "the health care system is fundamentally sound" and well enough funded.[4]

Canadians have confidence in "Medicare." They are committed to retention of the five principles of the Canada Health Act—universality, accessibility, portability, comprehensiveness, and public administration. Although none of these principles applies strictly, they apply with sufficient rigour that campaign talk about changing "Medicare" is the political equivalent of the "third rail."

The rest of the world looks on Canada as one of the best of countries in which to live. The United Nations' Human Development Report[5] has consistently rated Canada very highly, using measures that include three indices:

- Human Development—which is a composite of three variables, life expectancy, educational attainment, and real GDP per capita (expressed as purchasing power parity);

- Gender-related Development—the former index adjusted upward or down for gender inequality; and;

- Human Poverty—which measures human deprivation using such variables as the proportion of people expected to die before age forty, of adults who are illiterate, of underweight children under five years of age, and of people without access to health care services.

We know also that the health status of Canadians, measured by average life expectancy at birth, morbidity, and maternal and child mortality, incidence of "marker" diseases such as tuberculosis, malaria, and AIDS, and other related indicators, while not the best in the world, is good.

Therefore, relative to other countries and as measured by the satisfaction of the people served, the Canadian health **care** system, so-called, is in my opinion in very good to excellent shape.

But if we apply a cost-benefit analysis or, more generally, assess the state of the health **services** system against the whole spectrum of determinants that we know bear directly on the health status of the population, the report card is not as good. In other words, relative to other countries we are doing well. How well are we doing relative to what we could do?

Following the introduction of "Medicare," Canada's expenditures on health care services grew very rapidly and kept growing until the brakes were put on during this decade. Until recently we spent more of our resources on health care than any other nation with a publicly funded system; we were second only to the United States—cold comfort given the well-known problem of the uninsured in that country and the fact that the health status of Americans is not as good as ours.

Three things worry those paying attention:

- There is no correlation between spending on health care and the health of the population. Admittedly the measures are crude—longevity, maternal and infant mortality, etc., but the health of Britons (where 6 to 7 percent of GNP is spent on health care) is about the same as that of Canadians (we once spent 11.5 percent and now 9.7 percent[6]) or Americans (13.5 percent). At a recent international conference in Jakarta, the claim was made[7] that Costa Rica is the world's healthiest country, based on a new measure that calculates the ratio of life years produced relative to land and resources consumed; Costa Rica delivers seventy-six years of life expectancy on a national income of $1,850 per capita, compared with an average of seventy-seven years for the world's twenty-two richest countries with an average national income of $21,050. Are we spending our money as well as we can? Are we getting enough "health for the wealth"?

- Second, despite living since the Second World War in the best of economic times the developed world has known, Canada, its provinces, municipalities, and individuals ran deficits and built up a colossal debt that constitutes a big mortgage on our children's and grandchildren's future. To be blunt, we have lived beyond our means. It's time to pay and we are out of money.

- Third, the elderly require disproportionate amounts of health care. Canada's "baby boom," the largest in the developed world[8], will approach senior citizen status in the early 21st century. The present so-called health care system is simply incapable of meeting the anticipated need for health care services without bankrupting the nation.

The absence of correlation between how much is spent and the health of the population leads to a fourth point of concern:

- Spending so much on health care means less is available for other determinants of health such as care for the young, community and family support, education, housing, employment, the physical and social environment, and the support of healthier lifestyles. A landmark report in 1974 by the federal Department of Health and Welfare, *A New Perspective on the Health of Canadians*,[9] has been followed by increasingly compelling evidence[10] that these other determinants contribute far more to improving the health of the population than physicians, hospitals, and the whole panoply of health care services.

To answer the question, how good is Canada's health services system, you must ask also, good for what?

Our so-called system is good, excellent even, in ensuring access to the health care services provided by doctors and hospitals. It gets passable grades in providing access to drug therapy, home care, rehabilitation, and some forms of long-term care, but there are clearly two tiers in these categories of service; those who have private health insurance are substantially advantaged over those who do not.

But how good is the "system" if you define health as more than the absence of disease, something closer to the ideal articulated by the World Health Organization,[11] a resource for daily living?

The answer is unknown. We do know that there is no genuine, health services **system** in any Canadian province or territory. We suspect strongly that the individual elements of which such a system should be made are a lot less effective and more expensive than if we bridged the "silos" within health care and between health care and others of the major determinants of health, joined them together, and created a **real**, comprehensive health services system.

It is a simple fact of life that this will have to be done slowly and, in Canada, province by province. Health, education, and so many others of the policy fields bearing directly on health status are either exclusively or primarily provincial responsibilities. This raises, of course, the spectre of differences in the range of services offered and even of inequitable access to comparable services, province by province. But that exists now to some degree. Setting the risk of some inequity against the spectre of yet more constitutional wrangling about ways to prevent it, some differential access to health-related services is, in my opinion, by far the lesser evil.

The greatest threat to "Medicare," to the creation of a genuine health **care** system, and to the development of the more broadly-focused health **services** system we must create to face and meet the challenges of the early 21st century, is the absence of good data and information. Without the fruits of research on the productivity, including the cost-effectiveness of "Medicare," measured in terms of benefit to the health status of Canadians, we can only use our intuition on how to improve it. A great place to start would be with some sensitive, comprehensive measures of the health status of the population.

Without data and information on the need, as opposed to demand, for health services and the outcomes of their application, whether in hospital, through home care, in nursing homes, by physicians, nurses, rehabilitationists, or whomever, we cannot put in priority order the allocation of our scarce resources for the future. Without knowledge of how the many determinants of health interplay to affect the health of individuals and the population, we are flying blind, or at best in deep fog with only visual flight rules to guide us toward the most appropriate redesign of the provincial/territorial health services systems we really need.

To provide you with but one example, the Health Services Restructuring Commission in Ontario recently produced a discussion paper[12] in which it proposed some interim benchmarks that might be applied to necessary reinvestments of money from the hospital sector in home care, long-term care, mental health, rehabilitation care, and sub-acute care. Intuition predicts a strong correlation between decreasing length-of-stay in acute care hospitals and increasing home care services; there is no correlation whatsoever. There should be a very direct, predictable relationship between outpatient surgical procedures, cataract surgery for example, and home care; in fact, the use of home care following lens ablation ranges in Ontario's numerous home care districts from 2 percent to 96 percent and there are no studies to show which end of the spectrum leads to better outcomes.

It seems incredible that in the year 1997, in this educationally advanced country with the incredible technology available to us, we do not have a comprehensive information system firmly in place to support the effective operation of our most highly treasured and single most expensive social program.

It is a simple fact that a given patient can visit half a dozen physicians in a day, a hospital's emergency room, a chiropractor, an immunization clinic in the public health unit, and attend several pharmacies to fill prescriptions, and none of those concerned would know anything about the visits elsewhere unless the patient told them. It is also a simple fact that while we have very comprehensive data on patients who receive treatment in hospitals, we have very poor data on the far greater number who visit hospitals as ambulatory patients. Hospital records on patients are not available to the home care organizations or nursing homes or physicians or pharmacists who look after the same patients when they leave hospital. Simple data on credit card transactions yield far more comprehensive and timely information than is available on the so-called "system" on which the citizens of Ontario alone spend some $27 billion each year, and those of the country, $75 billion. If the ordinarily well-informed citizen were to know how parlous is the base of data and information available to support the planning and operation of our health care "system" she would have a fit!

What state are we in?

Despite all the talk about "cutbacks" in the last several years, the twelve health care systems in Canada are in good shape. They are meeting the people's needs in the 1990s and they are not "under-funded." The efficiencies that are being wrung out of them by hospital rationalization, regionalization, and other reforms will enable health care to cope through to the end of the century. But the status quo is not sustainable in the longer term, particularly as the population ages and the fiscal realities of balanced budgets remain, as they must.

Redesign of Canada's health care systems, and particularly their incorporation into genuine, comprehensive health **services** systems, must receive high priority now. We have to get ready for the 21st century.

Our greatest single need is for a comprehensive and powerful information system containing the data, information, and particularly the fruits of evidence-based research necessary to inform our intuition on how to meet the priority of creating a genuine health services system capable of meeting the challenges ahead.

Notes

1. Wilk, Martin B. 1991. *Health Information for Canada. Report of the National Task Force on Health Information.* p.2. "The Public Health is the foundation upon which rests the happiness of the people and the welfare of the nation." Attributed to Benjamin Disraeli.
2. The Concise Oxford Dictionary of Current English. 9th edition. Oxford: The Clarendon Press, 1995.
3. *sjukvard*
4. *Canada Health Action: Building on the Legacy. Final Report of the National Forum on Health.* 1997. Minister of Public Works and Government Services, Ottawa.
5. *Human Development Report.* United Nations Development Programme (UNDP). Oxford: Oxford University Press, 1997.

6. Canada's spending per capita on health/health care ranks 13th among developed nations. Raisa Deber. 1997. Personal communication.

7. Kickbusch, Ilona. 1997. *Think Health: What Makes the Difference?* 4th International Conference on Health Promotion, 21-25 July, Jakarta.

8. Foot, David K. with D. Stoffman. 1996. *Boom, Bust & Echo.* Toronto: Macfarlane, Walter and Ross.

9. *A New Perspective on the Health of Canadians* (Lalonde Report). Health and Welfare Canada. 1974. Information Canada, Ottawa.

10. Evans, R.G., M.L. Barer and T.R. Marmor (eds). 1994. *Why Are Some People Healthy and Others Are Not.* New York: Aldine de Grayter.

11. "Health is a state of complete physical, mental, and social well-being, and not merely the absence of disease and injury." *circa 1954.* World Health Organization. See Evans *et al.*, 28.

12. *Rebuilding Ontario's Health System: Interim Planning Guidelines and Implementation Strategies re Home Care, Long Term Care, Mental Health, Rehabilitation, and Sub-Acute Care.* 1997. Health Services Restructuring Commission, 56 Wellesley St. W., Toronto, Ontario M5S 2S3.

HENRY FRIESEN, FRSC

A Report Card on the Well-Being of Health Care Research in Canada: Choices to Be Made

Abstract

Repeated budget cuts to the Medical Research Council, which is the primary funder of health research in Canada, have obliged the Council to seek alternative sources of funding from the provinces and from industry, but even with such help the Council's budget is now reduced to the level of the early 1980s. This situation is the reverse of that of our G7 partners, who have been steadily increasing their funding for basic research. Health research has contributed immeasurably to the health and well-being of all Canadians, has permitted greater efficiency and economy in health care delivery, and has contributed to economic growth and job creation in Canada. Our widely admired health services system depends upon continuously funded basic research and is being threatened by short-sighted budget cuts.

Résumé

Les réductions maintes fois imposées au budget du Conseil de recherches médicales, le principal organe subventionnaire de la recherche médico-sanitaire au Canada, ont contraint ce dernier à chercher d'autres concours financiers de la part de provinces et du secteur privé, mais même là, son budget est désormais réduit à ce qu'il était au début des années 80. Cet état de choses est le contraire de ce qu'on observe chez nos partenaires du G7 qui n'ont jamais arrêté d'accroître le financement public de la recherche fondamentale. La recherche médico-sanitaire a apporté énormément à la santé et au bien-être de tous les Canadiens, elle a permis d'améliorer l'efficience et la rentabilité du secteur de la santé et elle a contribué à l'essor économique et à la création d'emplois au Canada. Notre système de santé publique, qui fait l'admiration générale, dépend du financement permanent de la recherche fondamentale, et il est donc compromis par les compressions budgétaires à courte vue.

Introduction

There is an old saying that a chain is only as strong as its weakest link. Well, basic research is fast becoming the weak link in the chain of health research, health care, and the knowledge economy.

The reason is simple: budget cuts that mean that, by 1998-99, the Medical Research Council (MRC), which is the primary funder of health research in Canada, will be operating with almost 17 per cent less money than we had at our peak in 1994-95. This puts our budget back to the levels of the early 1980s.

The budget cuts we have experienced on the face may seem modest—a bit one year, a bit more the next—but, taken together, they have added up to a very unstable foundation. As an experienced observer of the health research field, I have been forced to conclude that the health of the health research enterprise is in serious jeopardy.

These budget cuts placed an onus on the MRC to adapt and respond—and we did. We launched a strategic plan that expanded our role to encompass the full range of health research, and provided for partnerships and alliances with health-care providers, provinces, the voluntary sector, and, in particular, with industry.

These initiatives have been even more successful than we could have expected. Through our partnership with the Pharmaceutical Manufacturers' Association of Canada—the only program of its kind—$140 million of MRC peer-reviewed, industry-funded research investments have accrued in Canada.

Other partnerships include the Juvenile Diabetes Foundation and the Canadian Breast Cancer Research Initiative. All together, we have successfully levered every dollar we invest into $2.80 of outside funding. As a result, 25 percent more scientists are being funded than would otherwise be possible.

But there are limits to every success, and we are reaching the limits of this one. Every partnership we enter into, while generating new dollars for research, also requires dollars from our base budget—and that takes money away from our "core" business, basic research.

In this past year's competitions, the MRC had to turn down more than 500 wonderful proposals from talented research scientists in all parts of Canada, simply because we do not have the money. And even those scientists who are funded don't get enough money. Traditionally, our peer review panels have pared budgets in research proposals down to a bare minimum. Today, they still do that—but the Council then takes another 20 percent off the top, simply to keep more excellent laboratories open.

One of the most discouraging aspects of these cuts is that they fly in the face of what our G7 partners—and competitors—are doing. While our government has been cutting funding for basic research, other countries, including the United States, the United Kingdom, and France, have been increasing budgets—some by up to 40 percent. The National Institute of Health, our American counterpart, has five times as much money to spend per capita as the MRC—$40 compared to $8.

There have been some indications recently that the federal government may be placing more value on research. The establishment of the Canadian Health Services Research Foundation, the extension of permanent funding to the Networks of Centres of Excellence, the creation of the Canada Foundation for Innovation—all these are proof of a new perspective.

But the basic truth remains that all of these initiatives do not address the urgent need for investment in basic research. And without this investment, all other initiatives further up the discovery pipeline will not achieve their potential.

Underfunding basic research is short-sighted and self-defeating. Without immediate reinvestment in health research, the damage may well be irreparable. And that would harm Canadians, it would harm our health care system, it would harm this country's intellectual capital, and it would harm our economic growth and international competitiveness.

The Importance of Basic Health Research to the Health of Canadians

Health research has had a tremendous and direct impact on the health and well-being of Canadians.

For some people, research into the causes and prevention of disease has enabled them to avoid suffering from many different diseases and conditions.

For others, who have watched diseases such as Huntington's Chorea ravage their loved ones, health research has enabled them to learn whether their fetus carries the genes that would make it vulnerable to the same diseases—information without which they might have never contemplated starting a family.

For untold thousands of Canadians, health research has given them many more years in which to enjoy their friends and loved ones, because it has led to cures for diseases that were once considered fatal.

For others, those for whose diseases we have not yet discovered the cure—and I say "not yet" intentionally—health research is permitting them to live longer than they might have lived previously, and in greater comfort, thanks to progress on treatments that slow the progression of disease, if not stopping it entirely.

The fact is, health research has contributed immeasurably to the health and well-being of Canadians and of people around the world. From insulin to AIDS medication, Canadian health researchers have made the discoveries that have meant the difference between life and death.

The Importance of Basic Health Research to the Health Care System

If being able to keep Canadians healthy, and to ensure they receive the treatment they need when their health fails, has been a blessing for Canadians, it has been absolutely crucial to our health-care system.

In fact, health research lies at the basis of our health care system—which, despite what some naysayers may assert, remains one of the best in the world—and a strong health research base will help maintain and improve our health care system to carry us into the new century.

Health research has given us the information we need on a population basis to prevent disease and maintain health. It costs far less to prevent heart disease in a thousand Canadians, than to treat it in one.

Health research has led to the techniques that have permitted many surgeries, from gallbladder surgery to cataract operations, to be performed on a day-patient basis. Without this ability, governments could not even begin to consider the kind of restructuring in which Duncan Sinclair has been immersed over the past while.

Health services research can give us evidence as to how effective different treatments are, and about better, more cost-effective ways of delivering services to Canadians in areas like home care and primary care. And if we can get that equation right—delivering effective treatments in the most efficient way possible—then we will also be ensuring the maximum value for our health care dollar. And how do we determine what is effective? Not by pronouncement. Not by tradition. But by evidence, evidence generated through research.

Less than the best evidence is a waste. Taxpayers' hard-earned dollars should only be called on to underwrite that which has been proved effective and that proof is provided by appropriate research. That is at the heart of the call for an evidence-based health care system.

The Importance of Basic Health Research to the Development of Intellectual Capital

There is another aspect to health research, one common to all basic research training, whatever the field. Basic research trains young minds, creating the knowledge and skills that are essential for the quality of teaching in our educational system, from elementary to university, and for developing the multidimensional thinking and problem-solving abilities needed to respond to the complex challenges of the world we live in.

Through our system of funding basic research in Canada, we have here, as in many other parts of the world, an effective "apprenticeship" system where young scientists work with mentors in their laboratories before moving on to their own laboratories. This whole system, which ensures continuity and brings new minds to old problems, is endangered by the underfunding of basic research.

We have all heard about the brain drain. The impression I have received from meeting with my colleagues across the country is that the brain drain is possibly overstated. We do not have vast numbers of young scientists fleeing south of the border.

But certainly some scientists are leaving Canada to go where the opportunities are greater. And what we do not know is whether those who are going are the "best and the brightest". We also do not know how many potential scientists are lost at the beginning of the process, who are discouraged from entering the field by the dearth of opportunities they hear about.

The Importance of Basic Health Research to Our Economy

So far, I have talked about basic research as contributing to the health and well-being of individuals, as a basic foundation of our health-care system, and as a training ground for our intellectual capital. But, as I have certainly discovered during my tenure at the MRC, we academics are being forced to look beyond the ivory tower, and to deal more than ever before in "filthy lucre".

And what I have discovered is that health research is a burgeoning area of the economy, contributing to Canada's economic growth, to job creation, and to our international competitiveness.

There are eighty-two publicly traded companies in Canada in health sciences with a market value in 1996 of almost $12 billion. The largest, BioChem Pharma, has a market value of $3.1 billion, and more than 1,000 employees. Life sciences provide high-quality, well-paying employment to more than 70,000 people today, and this is forecast to rise to 125,000 by the year 2001.

And all of these companies have one thing in common, from BioChem Pharma to the newest and smallest of them all: none of them would exist were it not for the initial basic research, funded with grants from the MRC and other granting agencies.

That basic research leads to commercial discoveries isn't new. What is strikingly new is the entrepreneurial spirit that is accompanying these discoveries.

When I first discovered human prolactin, international companies very quickly capitalized on its diagnostic and therapeutic potential. As a result, a highly effective drug was developed that is now standard treatment around the world for infertile women who otherwise would not have experienced the joy and satisfaction of bearing children. In a vicarious sense, I share in their joy, and the thought that literally hundreds of thousands of children are alive today who otherwise would not have been.

Today's researchers think in terms of realizing commercial potential themselves. And they have the venture capital available to them to do so. In 1996, fully a quarter of all venture capital in Canada went to the life sciences—more than to any other sector, including computers, and a fivefold increase in the past three years.

And the single largest source of venture capital in the life sciences is individual Canadians, more than 70,000 of whom have seen the commercial potential of health research and have invested in Canadian Medical Discoveries Fund, a MRC-inspired initiative. I am proud to have played a small role in its creation.

In fact, it is my firm belief that the health sciences sector in Canada is in the same position the telecommunications sector was ten or twenty years ago—poised to take off to a degree of which we never could have dreamed a decade ago.

But unless we maintain the momentum that has driven this explosion in commercial activity—the momentum created by basic health research—the economic potential of the life sciences will never be released.

Conclusion

It is a law of science, as certain as any of Newton's laws, like gravity itself, that basic research is at the heart of all major breakthroughs in science and its applications. But commercial companies who are responsible to their shareholders, are not usually expected to make the long-term investment that basic research demands.

That is the role of government—to provide the necessary foundation to improve the health of Canadians, to maintain our health care system, to foster our intellectual capital, and to help stimulate economic growth and job creation.

One of the themes this seminar is exploring is the notion that it is easier to destroy than to build. Health research is a striking example of how true this is.

We have the basis for a fine system of basic health research in Canada. We have the infrastructure, and this is being renewed through the Canada Foundation for Innovation. We have committed and talented scientists.

We have an international reputation for excellence—a reputation that has consistently placed Canadian scientists in the top ten of the world's Scientific Citations Index. Our scientists produce 4 percent of the world's scientific output, in terms of research publications, and Canadian scientists rank number one in the world in terms of efficiency and impact of publications per dollar invested in research.

But this is all being put at risk, seemingly without much thought, by short-sighted budget cuts.

We are at a crisis point. If we do not see additional investment in basic research, we will soon see a system beyond easy repair.

It will take very little to destroy our system of health research in Canada. A few more years of the budget cuts we have been experiencing, a few more excellent research proposals that are turned down because of lack of money, a few more scientists opting to seek other, greener pastures—and before we know it, a system that has stood us in good stead for many years, a system that has benefited all, will have fallen into terminal disrepair.

But there is another choice: a conscious choice, to invest in health research in Canada. It will have to be a significant investment. It will have to be made for the long term. And, if it is made, it will benefit Canadians; it will benefit our health care system; it will benefit our intellectual capital; and it will benefit our economy.

But this choice is just wishful thinking without the political will to make it happen. And only those with the courage and vision to look at the longer term will be able to make it.

Short-sighted disrepair, or longer-term vision: the choice, to me, is clear.

URSULA M. FRANKLIN, FRSC

All Is Not Well in the House of Technology

Abstract

The paper draws attention to the lack of intellectual and methodological tools for the analysis of technology per se. Defining technology as practice, i.e., as "the way things are done", it becomes apparent that the domain of DOING, i.e., technology is much less well provided with instruments for survey and assessment than the domain of DECLARING, i.e., language and literature. In spite of the profound and structuring impact of technology on society, we know little about common and recurring attributes of technologies, of what would correspond to their language, grammar or syntax.

Résumé

Cette communication appelle l'attention sur l'absence d'outils intellectuels et technologiques pour l'analyse de la technologie en tant que telle. En définissant la technologie comme une façon de faire les choses, il devient vite évident que le domaine de l'ACTE, c'est-à-dire la technologie, est beaucoup moins bien doté d'instruments d'analyse et d'évaluation que le domaine du DIRE, en d'autres termes la langue et la littérature. En dépit de l'impact profond et structurant à la fois que la technologie a sur la société, nous en savons fort peu sur les attributs communs et répétitifs des technologies, ceux-là qui correspondraient à leur langage, à leur grammaire ou à leur syntaxe.

There is a certain amount of open-endedness in the title of this symposium, surely intended to allow the perspectives of different discussants to illuminate the theme.

My notion of the well-being of Canada is not expressed by GNP or international credit ratings, much as these measures may have their place in the scheme of things; even employment data, infant mortality statistics, income distributions or levels of pollution can convey to me only part of the picture of the well-being of a country. It is the degree of real hope and scope of the least powerful members of our society that is my indicator of the well-being of my country.

Having been asked to "examine how well Canada is doing in the area of technology", I realized that, had the President of the Academy of Science asked another of our members, this lecture might have begun with statistics on the number of computers, telephones or television sets in Canadian homes, or with the number and areas of high tech patents filed by Canadian inventors—and maybe the fate of such intellectual resources.

However, I do not intend to hand out merit or demerit points. Rather, I would like to look at "the area of technology" as both a field of specific knowledge and a field of general interest, because I want to emphasize those facets of the question to which we, as members of the Royal Society of Canada, might be able to make a contribution. We are, after all, intellectuals and academics for whom the temptation of analysing problems and coming to the conclusion that someone—not us—MUST do a. or b. and c. is always present. Yet, we do not need to yield to this temptation since there is something specific for US to do; I am convinced that the problems in what I call The House of Technology are not all "other people's problems".

This morning, I wish to argue that much of what is unwell in the House of Technology may be traced back to a lack of ACADEMIC and SCHOLARLY attention to technology per se. I also would like to make the case that Canadian scholars may be in a very good position to give such fresh and focused attention.

At this point, I need to define the term "technology" and my use of the term: I have always defined TECHNOLOGY as PRACTICE, i.e., as "the way things are done around here."[1]

This definition, while including all the elements of design, of devices and systems, of purpose and control, emphasizes that technology is a social phenomenon, not confined to the application of modern scientific knowledge. Technology, defined as culturally and socially rooted practice, is thus an integral part of every society. As a societal activity, technology—i.e., practice—is interactive, it involves and structures the collectivity; you can not have technology alone, just as you can not have literature alone (the very act of writing assumes a reader, separated from the writer in space and/or time).

Technologies have always been important to the well-being of societies, and yet there is a stunning discrepancy between the amount of intellectual attention, the level of methodological scrutiny, the extent of care and scholarship devoted to what people have DONE and how they have DONE "it", compared to what was SAID and WRITTEN.

There may be a great deal of talk about technology and technological change, but how much do we actually know about technology per se, or about the interactive structuring of society and technology?

Let me illustrate what I am trying to argue with the help of two drawings created a century apart.

The first one comes from a series of cards, commissioned by a French publishing house[2] in 1898 in order to illustrate life in the year 2000. The illustrator was asked to depict the changes in society under the impact of new and anticipated technologies. In this particular card we see "airmail" showing how the artist expects the new way of getting a letter from here to there to be implemented in the year 2000.

He evidently expected that this new way of doing something, this new technology, would not change anything else within the social fabric; it would be home delivery as usual, probably twice a day.

The cartoon on the second overhead comes from a flyer advertising a public meeting on technological unemployment in Toronto in November 97.[3] A librarian, presiding over a room full of readers, each sitting in front of an individual video display terminal, answers an inquiry with " Sir, this is a library; if you want a book, go to a book store."

Here, again, is a new technology applied to an established activity ... but can we assume that "there will be public libraries as usual" in the manner in which a hundred years ago an artist assumed that there would be home delivery of letters in the year 2000. If we do NOT believe any more that one social practice, one technology, can be changed without effecting other social practices, how do we study, describe or assess the interplay of technologies in general and systemic terms?

If we were to imagine the interdependent technologies as rooms in a house, connected by doorways and corridors, then I hold that this House of Technology is not well lit: it seems to be full of trap doors, lacking exits and windows, and, most of all, signs or direction indicators.

Although we live in a country—and in a world—that is increasingly and rapidly restructured by new practices, by new technologies, we have few if any intellectual tools to address technology as a social force—not in terms of good, bad or indifferent, but in terms of its attributes, statements and internal consistencies or inconsistencies. Yet without analytical tools and methodologies, it is almost impossible to contemplate an answer to the question "How well is Canada doing with respect to technology?"

In other words, I would argue that nothing has had a greater impact on the events of the past hundred years than changes in technology. There have been dramatically novel and different practices used to accomplish what one might call the basic tasks of civilization. These tasks have really not changed profoundly over the millennia: human communities have always tried to provide food and shelter for their members, direction and instruction for the young, myths and signposts that validate their traditions, safety, care and scope for the collectivity.

What has changed so profoundly over time is HOW these tasks have been and are being carried out. Advances in knowledge or access to new resources have been translated into new practices, new ways of doing the task at hand. Yet where do we turn for an analysis of these technologies? It seems to me that we cannot inform ourselves on technology as technology as we can, for instance, on literature as literature, on language as language.

The domain of "doing"—its context and its actors—has not had the degree of intellectual illumination that the domain of "declaring"—the world of the spoken and written word, with its context, rules and meanings has had.

There may be historical reasons for this lack of systematic scholarship of technology as a field of inquiry: the Euro-centred emphasis on LITERACY in education, compared to CONDUCT and ACTION, may have something to do with it. But whatever the roots of this imbalance in transparency, it needs to be addressed.

There is, I would suggest to you, a new and major field of scholarship in the making, a field that is transdisciplinary more than interdisciplinary, because it will cut across the traditional boundaries of disciplines and academic faculties. Its new knowledge, while building on scholarship and insights of existing fields, will transform and extend in scope and method the inquiry into the nature of technology.

I am conscious of the contributions made already. No one will labour in this area of study without being influenced and stimulated by Mumford[4], Foucault[5], Bertalanffy[6], Ellul[7] and many others. Particularly the notions of technology as a system, or Ellul's concepts of technology as "milieu", have influenced thinkers and practitioners alike.

But we are still, I feel, without adequate methodologies to analyse technology in general terms. I would like to indicate how the mapping strategies of other disciplines might provide fruitful morphological parallels for the work of those concerned about the structure of technology.

Why not look at technology as TEXT.

We all are aware of the simultaneous presence of declaring and doing, of word and deed in our lives. We have the artifacts of the word as well as the scholarship to evaluate and critique the written record. But we also have the artifacts of the deed, the physical, social and institutional evidence of technologies past and present, though only a much less developed scholarship of analysis and critique.

Think, for a moment, of the introduction of a new technology as DOING a text. Looked upon as a TEXT, does a given technology, a particular practice, not have substantiative and/or relational components in its "language"? Surely there are also subtexts and assumptions here, just as there is context, meaning, consistency or inconsistency to be discerned in any technological process or activity.

In my own work, I have put forward the general distinction between holistic and prescriptive technologies, but there is so much more to be done to discern the recurring elements, the words and the vocabulary of technology. We need grammar, syntax and structure as well as the signs and the symbolic components of technology as text and/or language.

In the past, technology has been "read" by those who commented on it, including myself, mainly as social instruction, the how-to manual that outlines a task and its context. Now it is time to read and interpret technology as literature, as text per se. It is no longer solely a matter of content, but also one of an analysis of the constituent elements, both visible and implied.

In the examples that follow I have tried to indicate how one might approach a textual analysis of technology. Carrying out such a new methodological work is obviously beyond the reach of my own scholarship. The examples and their discussion are intended mainly to stimulate my colleagues, who master different intellectual instruments, to look again at the discourse about technology.

Let me assure you that I am not trying to revisit the debates about structures in literature and science[8,9] or the discussions on ways of knowing.[10,11] What I am wrestling with is the need for an anatomy of technology that could stand in a point-counterpoint relationship to the anatomy of literature—in the broadest sense of the term.

As I try to understand the world of technology I am grappling with the lack of intellectual tools and look to the humanities for help. The domain of DOING requires the mapping and orienteering instruments that the world of DECLARING begins to take for granted. It may, in the end, turn out to be a quest for an appropriate taxonomy.

My first example relates to the ski lift. When I came to Canada I was astonished to see the effects of rather severe skiing accidents among my fellow post docs. Though I had skied in Germany, I had never known ski lifts and it took me a while to see the link between the availability of a lift and the severity of the accidents encountered on the down path. Quite simply, the process of getting up a slope without mechanical help seems to convey skills that are adequate to get down reasonably safely. Mechanizing the "up" part of the practice changed the risks of the "down" part.

How might one analyse this simple change in technology as a DOING TEXT?

There is a TASK, the plot, the story: to get up to a certain point on a mountain and down again. There is an ACTIVITY associated with the task, i.e., to do the climb and descend on skis.

The prerequisite for the activity, in addition to the trivial ones such as having skis, a mountain, snow, etc., are skiing skills as well as some skills of informed observation, assessment, collaboration.

The text may be divided into two parts, Chapter 1, the ascent, Chapter 2, the descent and we have two versions before us: the Pedestrian version, in which the task is carried out without mechanical assistance and the Ski Lift version in which the ascent is mechanized.

The task remain the same in both versions, but in the Ski Lift version the ascent is accomplished externally. Something different, another actor, another voice, tense or language has come into the Ski Lift version.

This change does not affect the task level of the text; the ascent is readily accomplished. The change in technology, though, does affect the activity and skill level of the text. It becomes clear that although the task in Chapter 1 can be more readily completed with the help of the new technology, the very use of an external mechanism diminishes the activity and skill content of Chapter 1 in the Ski Lift Version.

Chapter 2, the descent, is the same in both versions as far as task and activity are concerned. Yet in terms of context and form, there is a significant discontinuity (might it be in vocabulary, language, grammar or syntax?) between Chapter 1 and Chapter 2 of the Ski Lift version, a discontinuity that is not apparent in the Pedestrian version, where Chapter 1 and Chapter 2 seem to flow without a break (pardon the pun) in either the skill or the activity levels (subtexts?).

Actually DOING Chapter 1 in the Pedestrian Version confers skills required TO DO Chapter 2. The Ski Lift Version, though lacking the activity that allows the acquisition of the necessary skills, implicitly assumes their presence.

A textual analysis would notice the changes in voice (style, grammar) as well as the new unstated and possibly unwarranted assumptions. One could request clarification through footnotes or other editorial devices in order to draw attention to the significant changes between apparently identical texts (plots).

This discussion is not intended as an argument against ski lifts but a plea for clarity, using as case in point a simple and transparent illustration. Yet any good analysis of a simple situation ought to identify structural elements, signifiers of discontinuities or conceptual gaps, that could be transferred to more general and complex considerations.

In my second example, I would like to extend the ski lift analysis to the much more complex situation of external aids to teaching and learning, i.e., to the realm of the development and transfer of knowledge and understanding.

Of course, there have always been external aids to teaching and learning, books and dictionaries, mathematical tables, charts and slide rules. But the scope and capacity of modern computers and their linking must be seen as much more than a vast increase in the number of standard aids and their uses. The structure of teaching and learning has so changed that we may want to examine the new text of education and compare it to the previous version.

For the sake of transparency, I would like to confine myself to certain aspects of education in a school setting, in particular the introduction of electronic spellers and calculators or their equivalents into the classroom.

Looking at the situation as a TEXT, one can again discern a specific task: the mastery of spelling or the competence to carry out a mathematical operation. As before, the tasks involve an activity level (i.e., learning) and a skill component (i.e., applying what has been learned).

The specific tasks arise within a larger context, be it writing and composition, be it setting and solving numerical or mathematical problems. As in the ski lift case, part of the larger task can be accomplished today by external devices.

Therefore the consequences of the task-related skills, i.e., spelling or calculating correctly, come into use in spite of bypassing the task-related activities, i.e., learning how to spell or calculate correctly.

One of the questions arising from the new technological possibilities is this: how is the overall text, its content, its internal logic and consistency, its credibility and conclusions affected by the external task substitutions and transpositions? To answer these questions, we will have to go back to the main TEXT of education in which the specific tasks are embedded.

In the context of this analysis I will define the purpose of classroom education as the growth of the students' knowledge and understanding. Thus the tasks of spelling and calculating correctly are only part of the overall plot/story of the text.

In the ski lift case, mechanizing the ascent may leave the skier with inadequate skills for a safe descent; the classroom case is similar, though less transparent. The activities related to learning how to spell and calculate teach more than mastering the tasks at hand. They include implicit lessons for the student on how to work in a group and to learn how to learn, as well as lessons in tolerance and anger management, in inventiveness and response. Such implicit social learning has to be accomplished, even if the explicit tasks of spelling and calculating can be relegated forever to external devices.

Physical injuries resulting from the imprudent use of ski lifts can be identified relatively easily and remedial measures can be undertaken. But do we have to await potential social injuries and their tracing back to changes in explicit and implicit learning, before discussing the new teaching technologies or supplementing them with new sources of skills?

Can one not analyse the changes in "syntax" of the new text of education—as text—to illuminate its structure, gaps or discontinuities and compare this text to other texts with similar plots/stories?

Other examples that I could give you, such as the use of electronic communications and transactions[12], are of greater complexity, but I could see them being analysed and discussed in terms of elements and motives identifiable in the simpler cases.

And here again comes my plea to colleagues in the humanities for their help. Serious methodological research into technology as text would be brain intensive, but not capital intensive. It would promote a new kind of inter- and transdisciplinarity and encourage a fundamental approach to our most relevant problems.

Canada, as a country, could provide many examples for such a textual analysis of technology, examples of new practices, novel ways of doing things as well as of their structuring impacts. Such examples might range from roads vs. railways to radio, telephone, fax and Internet penetration of both the North and the southern parts of our country. Both the French and the English language analysis of the realm of "declaring" is well represented among our colleagues and I am confident that they will be able to adapt their scholarship to the realm of "doing".

I am also sure that this Society will welcome the practitioners of the new discipline and will even come to a decision about which of our Academies they should belong to.

Notes

1. Franklin, U.M. *The Real World of Technology*. Toronto: House of Anansi Press, 1990.
2. Azimov, Isaac. (illustrations by Jean Mark Cote) *Futuredays*, London: Virgin Books, 1986.
3. Coalition against Technological Unemployment. Toronto, 1997.
4. Mumford, Lewis, *The Myth of the Machine:Technics and Human Development*. New York: Harcourt Brace Jovanovich, 1967.
5. Foucault, Michel. *The Order of Things*, New York: Random House, 1970.
6. Bertalanffy, Ludwig von. *General System Theory*, New York: Braziller, rev.1973.
7. Ellul, Jacques. *The Technological Society*. New York: Knopf 1964. *The Technological System,* New York: Continuum, 1980.
8. see for instance " *Chaos and Order; Complex Dynamics of Literature and Science* , N.Katherine Hayles ed. Chicago: University of Chicago Press, 1991 particularly the Editor's introduction.
9. Latour, Bruno. *Science in Action*. Milton Keynes: U.K. Open University Press, 1987.
10. Bateson, Gregory. *Steps to an Ecology of Mind*. New York: Ballantine, 1972.
11. Poulson, William R. *The Noise of Culture*. Ithaca: Cornell University Press, 1988.
12. Franklin U.M. *Every Tool Shapes Its Task*. Vancouver, Chapbooks 1997.
    ——————— "Beyond the Hype", *Leadership in Health Services* vol. 5, no 4, July/August 1996, pp. 14-18.

GISÈLE PAINCHAUD

L'éducation au ban des accusés

Résumé

Depuis le début des années quatre-vingt, l'éducation subit une remise en question par le monde des affaires, les décideurs politiques et les médias. Les critiques portent sur la qualité de la formation, le taux de diplomation au secondaire et le niveau de financement optimal dans le cadre de la crise des finances publiques. Les attentes à l'égard de l'éducation vont dans le sens d'un rehaussement des exigences pour assurer la formation des ressources humaines dans le contexte de la société du savoir et de la compétitivité internationale. Des réformes en cours dans la plupart des provinces en matière de curriculum et de réaménagements organisationnels montrent que l'éducation au Canada connaît une réorientation vers les standards internationaux qui sont en train de s'imposer, tout en tenant compte de la spécificité de la société canadienne.

Abstract

Since the early eighties, education has been under fire by business leaders, politicians and the media. Education is being questioned as to the quality and relevance of its curriculum, the proportion of students who graduate from high school and its high level of funding in this period of governmental downsizing. Education is expected to upgrade the competencies of high school graduates in order to ensure that human resources will be better prepared to face the challenge of the knowledge society and its corollary, international competitiveness, and to better respond to the needs of a pluralist society. Most provinces have initiated major reforms in areas such as curriculum and organization of the educational system. These transformations should be viewed in the context of the internationalization of education and the uniqueness of Canadian society.

L'éducation scolaire est une entreprise sociale vouée à la promotion de va-
leurs largement partagées par la collectivité et à la poursuite de buts
sociétaux (McEwen, 1995). Comme la santé, l'éducation constitue un domaine majeur de dépenses publiques, mais là s'arrête la comparaison.

La responsabilité juridique, administrative et financière de l'éducation in-
combe aux dix provinces et aux territoires. Il y a donc, au Canada, non pas
un seul mais bien douze systèmes d'éducation. Au cours de l'année
1994-1995, 35,1 milliards de dollars ont été consacrés à l'enseignement
primaire et secondaire, ce qui représente 62% du budget total réservé à
l'éducation au Canada (Lawton, 1996). Le Canada compte plus de cinq
millions d'élèves dans ses 16 000 écoles primaires et secondaires (Dunning, 1997). L'ampleur de cette gigantesque entreprise peut aussi se voir
par le nombre d'enseignants et d'enseignantes œuvrant au sein des écoles.
Selon Statistique Canada (Tremblay, 1997), 346 088 enseignants (équiva-
lence temps plein) auraient travaillé au cours de la semaine de référence
d'octobre 1995.

Devant cet investissement considérable pour l'éducation obligatoire, celle
qui va de l'éducation préscolaire au diplôme d'études secondaires, soit les
12 ou 13 premières années de scolarisation, il n'étonne pas que la population et les pouvoirs publics s'interrogent sur le fonctionnement de
l'éducation, les résultats obtenus et la pertinence de la préparation que
reçoivent les jeunes pour l'avenir de la société canadienne. L'éducation est
de plus en plus disséquée, évaluée et critiquée, surtout depuis qu'il est
avéré que l'apport des ressources humaines, le capital cognitif, est la variable cruciale de l'avenir des sociétés. Depuis le début des années
quatre-vingt, dans la foulée du rapport américain intitulé *A Nation at Risk*,
l'éducation a été placée sous haute surveillance par le monde des affaires,
les décideurs politiques et les médias. L'éducation ne serait pas à la hauteur
des attentes de la société faute d'avoir su s'adapter assez rapidement aux
exigences des sociétés technologisées et ouvertes au commerce international. Le bien-être de notre société en serait même compromis, si tant est
que le potentiel humain que constitue la population en âge scolaire ne serait
pas suffisamment développé.

De telles allégations sont certes graves à l'ère de la société du savoir et
pourraient même justifier une enquête pour examiner plus attentivement
les faits et essayer, si faire se peut, d'identifier le ou les coupables. L'éducation passe donc des bancs de l'école au ban des accusés.

Avant d'entendre la cause, il faut d'abord clarifier davantage la nature des critiques adressées à l'éducation.

Que reproche-t-on précisément à l'éducation?

Premièrement, la qualité de l'éducation est suspecte. Les diplômés du secondaire ne sont pas formés adéquatement pour le marché du travail. De plus, le diplôme d'études secondaires ne comporte pas de garantie de qualité uniforme, les niveaux de compétence des diplômés pouvant varier d'une province à l'autre et même à l'intérieur d'une même juridiction scolaire. L'éducation n'est pas encore à l'heure de la qualité totale.

Deuxièmement, le taux de diplomation à la fin du secondaire n'est pas suffisamment élevé. Une trop grande proportion des jeunes quittent l'école sans diplôme. Une société comme la nôtre doit permettre à tous les jeunes d'obtenir le diplôme d'études secondaires. L'efficacité de l'éducation doit donc être améliorée.

Troisièmement, en comparaison des pays du G7, le Canada se situe en première place pour le coût moyen par élève. C'est là un domaine dans lequel le Canada ne souhaite pas être premier de classe puisqu'il se situe plutôt dans la bonne moyenne pour le reste.

Dans une société axée sur la compétence, le capital cognitif, la productivité et la compétitivité, des manquements à la qualité, l'efficacité et l'efficience sont à n'en pas douter des fautes majeures qu'il faut à tout prix corriger.

Il reste à appeler les témoins à la barre pour pouvoir juger du bien-fondé de ces allégations et examiner les circonstances atténuantes qui pourraient permettre d'expliquer comment le monde de l'éducation pourrait se situer à ce point à contre-courant de la société canadienne.

Les témoins à charge

L'alerte au sujet de la piètre performance de l'éducation provient de trois sources différentes : le monde des affaires, les décideurs politiques et les médias.

Le monde des affaires

Des critiques se sont d'abord manifestées au sujet des capacités dites ina-
déquates des diplômés du secondaire. À la suite d'une enquête auprès
d'entreprises, Deslauriers (1990) constatait que les employeurs étaient in-
satisfaits des compétences en lecture et en écriture des nouveaux diplômés
qui entraient sur le marché du travail. De façon générale, le niveau de
maîtrise de la langue laissait beaucoup à désirer, que ce soit pour la lecture
ou pour l'écriture. Pour que ces nouveaux employés soient mieux en mesure d'exécuter les tâches qui leur étaient confiées, des entreprises ont
même dû se résoudre à offrir une formation de base, une responsabilité qui
relève clairement de l'école. Devant la constatation que l'école ne remplis-
sait pas sa mission de préparation au marché du travail, le Conference
Board du Canada a défini en 1992 le profil des compétences relatives à
l'employabilité que devraient à l'avenir posséder les diplômés du secondaire. Plus récemment sont mises de l'avant les compétences en sciences,
technologies et mathématiques. Emportés dans la tourmente de la globalisation, de la compétitivité internationale et du changement perpétuel
alimenté par les technologies de l'information et de la communication, les
gens d'affaires prônent avec insistance une éducation centrée sur le
développement des compétences requises pour une meilleure intégration
au marché du travail. De plus en plus, on avance que sans un diplôme
d'études secondaires, il est presque assuré que l'avenir doit s'entrevoir
d'emplois précaires, de chômage et de bas revenus.

Sur la base des résultats de leurs travaux de recherche, les experts corro-
borent pour l'essentiel le rehaussement des exigences dont fait état le
monde des affaires aussi bien pour l'insertion sur le marché du travail que
pour les besoins ultérieurs de formation continue (Jezak, Painchaud, d'Anglejan et Temisjian, 1995).

Les décideurs politiques

La fin de l'État providence et la crise des finances publiques ont amené les
décideurs politiques à scruter à la loupe les allocations budgétaires, princi-
palement dans les domaines qui accaparent une forte proportion des
dépenses publiques, soit la santé, l'éducation et l'assistance sociale. L'éducation, qui est de responsabilité provinciale, s'est trouvée dans la mire, à
cause de la part substantielle qu'elle représente dans les dépenses gouver-
nementales. Puis, les comparaisons interprovinciales et internationales sur

le pourcentage de dépenses que représentait l'éducation par rapport à l'ensemble du budget ou au produit national brut (PNB), incluant le coût moyen par élève, ont permis de mettre en perspective des données qui, jusque-là, étaient considérées de manière absolue. Très rapidement, la conclusion s'est imposée : au total, le Canada dépense davantage que les pays du G7 pour l'éducation. Toutes dépenses confondues, le Canada consacre plus de 7% de son PNB à l'éducation, davantage que les États-Unis, l'Australie, l'Allemagne et le Japon (OCDE, Conference Board). Cependant, c'est pour l'éducation post-secondaire que le Canada se situe en tête du peloton. De ceci, il ressort que la société canadienne consacre autant de ressources, sinon plus, que les autres pays au financement de l'éducation.

La question de l'efficience a suivi : les résultats obtenus correspondent-ils à l'investissement consenti? Là encore la réponse a été brutale. Le taux de diplomation, qui se situe présentement autour de 82% (Statistique Canada, 1993) avec des variations importantes dans la répartition des données entre les provinces, est jugé trop faible. Une déperdition de 18% des élèves du groupe d'âge susceptible de terminer les études secondaires, correspondrait à condamner ces jeunes à la pauvreté à vie et surtout à les priver de la possibilité de poursuivre leur formation par la suite. Il est bien connu qu'en ce qui concerne la scolarisation, la consommation croit avec l'usage. Le Conference Board avait estimé en 1992 que la perte financière et économique occasionnée par les abandons scolaires pour la cohorte de 1989 se situait à quatre milliards. Ce sont des chiffres qui parlent d'eux-mêmes.

Les résultats d'enquêtes internationales ont également permis de mieux situer les résultats obtenus par les systèmes scolaires du Canada en lecture, en sciences et en mathématiques. Les résultats de ces enquêtes qui ont été largement médiatisés sont difficiles à interpréter à cause des différences provinciales et internationales dans le curriculum, du taux de fréquentation scolaire du groupe d'âge visé et des degrés divers d'hétérogénéité des populations scolaires (Nagy, 1996). Il n'en reste pas moins que, dans l'ensemble, le Canada se compare assez bien, quoiqu'il n'ait jamais les notes les plus élevées. Pour la lecture et l'écriture, il est rassurant de constater que les jeunes obtiennent de meilleurs résultats que les plus âgés, mais que subsiste encore une trop forte proportion d'entre eux qui n'atteignent pas les niveaux de compétence requis pour les emplois de l'avenir. Parmi les jeunes âgés de 16 à 29 ans, 12,5% se situent au niveau le plus bas de la compétence évaluée par l'échelle et 22,9%, au niveau suivant, une compétence qui n'est pas non plus suffisante pour assurer l'employabilité, d'après les données de l'Enquête internationale sur l'alphabétisation des adultes (Statistics Canada, 1996). Il y a donc encore plus du tiers de ce groupe d'âge qui ne possède pas le niveau correspondant à la fin des études secondaires. C'est pourtant mieux que les Etats-Unis (43,7%) et comparable à l'Allemagne (34,7%), mais bien en deçà des résultats obtenus par la Suède (18%).

Depuis la présente décennie, le Conseil des ministres de l'éducation du Canada a joué un rôle de coordination dans l'établissement d'indicateurs de rendement de l'éducation. L'évaluation des élèves de 13 et de 16 ans en mathématiques, en sciences et en lecture et écriture contribuent à fournir des données sur le rendement scolaire des élèves canadiens. Pour les élèves de 6ᵉ année en mathématiques, les données préliminaires permettent de dire que les facteurs sexe et situation socio-économique influent peu sur la réussite des élèves. Comme l'éducation vise l'égalité des chances en matière de réussite scolaire, il est rassurant de constater qu'au moins en mathématiques au primaire, il est possible de faire valoir qu'il y a adéquation entre les objectifs poursuivis et les résultats obtenus.

Les médias

Les médias concourent à entretenir ce sentiment de crise en éducation en faisant état des situations problèmes dans le système d'éducation, qu'il s'agisse des résultats scolaires concernant différentes matières,de la violence à l'école, des conflits inter-groupes, des difficultés des écoles en milieux socio-économiquement faibles, des revendications des enseignants et des parents, etc., bref des problèmes, nous en convenons tous, qui sont ceux de la société ordinaire. L'école ne saurait être que le miroir de la société dans laquelle elle évolue et, pour cette raison, elle se doit d'incarner la vision idéale de la société.

L'image qui ressort dans les médias est celle d'une école qui tarde à s'adapter à la société du savoir, une école qui n'arrive plus à satisfaire les besoins de tous ces jeunes qui la fréquentent, une école déshumanisée et bureaucratisée, dans laquelle les jeunes se sentent de plus en plus étrangers. À l'occasion, il est fait état de projets innovateurs, d'écoles qui, en dépit de circonstances difficiles, obtiennent de très bons résultats, d'enseignantes et d'enseignants compétents et engagés, mais c'est l'exception.

D'après ces témoignages, la préparation des élèves pour le travail ne répond pas vraiment aux attentes des entreprises, les résultats obtenus ne correspondent pas au financement alloué et l'écart entre les aspirations des élèves et l'école tend à augmenter. Puisque l'éducation est considérée comme un investissement à long terme dans le bien-être futur et la prospérité du Canada, qu'on cherche à trouver les responsables de cette situation souvent qualifiée de préoccupante montre que l'éducation demeure un objet de débat et un enjeu démocratique de premier plan.

Reste maintenant à entendre les témoins de la défense qui sont les acteurs engagés dans le processus d'éducation, le personnel scolaire, les parents et les élèves.

Le personnel scolaire

Le personnel scolaire, avec les parents et les élèves, contribue à la réalisation de l'entreprise éducative. Mais l'éducation étant un domaine normatif, il s'avère impossible d'établir un consensus sur presque tous les aspects de son fonctionnement. C'est la constatation à laquelle est arrivée la Commission royale sur l'éducation de l'Ontario (1994) et, dans une moindre mesure, la Commission des états généraux sur l'éducation (1996) au Québec. Les finalités de l'éducation sont plurielles et ne sont pas partagées également par l'ensemble des intervenants. A des degrés divers, tous les systèmes éducatifs visent le développement des capacités intellectuelles et culturelles, la préparation à l'exercice d'une citoyenneté responsable, la maîtrise de compétences professionnelles pour assurer l'insertion sur le marché du travail et l'actualisation du potentiel de l'élève, soit l'épanouissement des élèves. Il est intéressant de faire remarquer que le Québec, après avoir mis l'accent sur le développement intégral de l'élève, vient d'imprimer de nouvelles orientations au système d'éducation (Enoncé de politique, 1997), autour de trois missions présentées dans l'ordre suivant : instruire, socialiser et qualifier.

D'autres tensions viennent exacerber ces diverses représentations des missions de l'école. Au Canada, la fréquentation obligatoire a fait en sorte que l'école soit à la longue accessible à tous les enfants du groupe d'âge visé par la loi de chacune des provinces. La fréquentation est présentement de 100% (Tremblay, 1997), ce qui signifie que l'école accueille des enfants qui présentent des caractéristiques intellectuelles, physiques et ethnoculturelles fort diverses. Dans la même école, et souvent dans la même classe, peuvent se trouver des élèves doués, d'autres avec des difficultés d'apprentissage ou des incapacités physiques ou intellectuelles et, dans les grands centres urbains comme Montréal, Toronto et Vancouver, d'origines ethnoculturelles variées. Faire en sorte que tous ces élèves aient des chances égales de réussite scolaire suppose une inégalité de traitement pour que chacun puisse effectivement actualiser son potentiel. La réussite pour tous dans un tel contexte de diversité pose des défis que la pédagogie différenciée n'a pas encore entièrement résolus. Le décrochage et des résultats scolaires plus faibles sont des symptômes de la difficulté qu'éprouve l'école à transiger avec ces réalités, qui sont relativement nouvelles, et qui découlent du pluralisme de la société canadienne. Auparavant, il paraissait normal d'accepter l'échec scolaire. L'importance accrue que la société accorde à la qualification minimale de la main-d'œuvre et à la reconnaissance du droit à une éducation de base pour tous les citoyens fait en sorte que la réussite de tous les élèves relève maintenant de l'école. Ce virage, qui s'est effectué au cours des dernières années, doit être qualifié de majeur. On est passé de l'adaptation de l'élève à l'école à l'adaptation de l'école à l'élève, un changement de paradigme dans la manière de concevoir et de dispenser l'éducation.

Les enseignants détiennent, dans leur très grande majorité, un baccalauréat et ont reçu la formation requise pour l'obtention de la certification décernée par chacune des provinces. N'entre pas qui veut à l'école.

Leur fonction est exigeante et ne saurait être réduite au temps de présence en salle de classe comme leurs détracteurs le laissent souvent entendre. Le contexte dans lequel les enseignants évoluent est devenu difficile. Les jeunes auxquels ils s'adressent sont de plus en plus issus de familles aux prises avec de dures réalités : le chômage des parents, le manque de disponibilité lorsque les deux parents travaillent, la monoparentalité, l'appauvrissement, etc. L'école et les enseignants doivent également suppléer au manque de soutien apporté historiquement par d'autres institutions sociales qui sont elles-mêmes affaiblies : la famille, l'église, la communauté, notamment en milieu urbain.

Pour les enseignants, la prise en compte de toute cette diversité au sein d'une même classe exige des habiletés professionnelles de haut niveau.

L'adaptation à des besoins fort différents nécessite que les élèves plus forts maintiennent leur intérêt tout en permettant aux élèves plus faibles de continuer à faire les apprentissages requis.

Les enseignants, trop souvent dévalorisés socialement et confrontés à tous ces problèmes sociaux avec lesquels l'école est aux prises, éprouvent un profond malaise qui peut aller jusqu'à l'épuisement professionnel et la fatigue mentale. Les enseignants, plus encore que les policiers et les infirmières, se retrouvent en plus forte proportion en situation d'invalidité (Dionne-Proulx, 1995).

Les enseignants souhaitent à la fois la participation des parents à l'école et hésitent à les y inviter de crainte de les voir empiéter sur leur autonomie professionnelle.

Les parents

Le rôle des parents à l'école est fort variable selon les époques et selon les lieux. Leur influence est grande lorsqu'ils choisissent de se manifester, mais leur présence se limite souvent aux rencontres formelles prévues au cours de l'année avec les enseignants.

De façon générale, ils sont assez satisfaits de l'école. La plupart des sondages sur le niveau de satisfaction du public à l'endroit de l'éducation montrent que les parents estiment que l'école que fréquentent leurs enfants est une bonne école. C'est là une constante maintes fois vérifiée. Les parents contrairement au public en général, ont une meilleure connaissance du fonctionnement de l'école et peuvent en conséquence porter un jugement plus éclairé.

En revanche, la participation des parents aux activités de l'école et aux travaux scolaires des enfants varie en fonction du niveau socio-économique de la famille, les parents plus scolarisés montrant davantage d'intérêt. Les rapports avec l'école sont plus fréquents pour les élèves du début du primaire que par la suite, les élèves plus âgés étant sans doute considérés plus aptes à s'occuper eux-mêmes de leurs études.

Des études révèlent qu'il y a un lien entre le degré de participation des parents dans les programmes de l'école et les comportements scolaires et sociaux de l'enfant. (Fortin et Mercier, 1994). Conscient de l'influence qu'exercent les parents sur le rendement des élèves, le personnel des établissements scolaires favoriserait de plus en plus le développement d'un ensemble d'habiletés parentales susceptibles d'améliorer le cheminement scolaire des élèves.

Dans certains milieux, les parents ont revendiqué et obtenu d'exercer un rôle collectif à l'école, mais il s'agit d'une minorité participante (Proulx, 1997). Par contre, il semble que les parents aient un intérêt certain pour la vie scolaire de leurs enfants et ils se disent favorables à une formation pour les aider à superviser les devoirs et les leçons (Saint-Laurent, Royer, Hébert et Tardif, 1994).

Les élèves

Comme usagers et bénéficiaires des services éducatifs, les élèves sont polyphones. Ils se répartissent entre ceux qui persévèrent aux études et ceux qui quittent l'école.

Les élèves qui terminent leurs études sont plutôt satisfaits de leur parcours scolaire, des enseignants et des activités étudiantes (Hart, Deblois, Castonguay, 1994). Il est même surprenant de constater qu'ils souhaitent un rehaussement des exigences scolaires (Commission des états généraux sur l'éducation, 1996). La très grande majorité d'entre eux déclarent se sentir à l'aise à l'école (Cloutier, 1991).

Les élèves qui abandonnent l'école avant l'âge prévu ou qui quittent l'école dès le moment où ils ne sont plus obligés de la fréquenter, sont ceux qui attirent le plus l'attention des éducateurs et des pouvoirs publics. Les motifs de l'abandon scolaire sont connus : le faible rendement scolaire, l'ennui à l'école, la perception de l'inutilité des cours, la consommation de drogues et d'alcool, l'inimitié envers les enseignants, le rejet de la discipline imposée à l'école, etc. (Hrimech et Théoret, 1997). La mise en œuvre de programmes de dépistage, d'intervention précoce et de raccrochage, sont les moyens les plus fréquemment utilisés pour augmenter la persévérance. Valorisant faiblement les études, ces élèves ébranlent les fondements mêmes de l'école comme institution sociale. Ce sont ceux qui, en définitive, la contestant, contribuent le plus à sa rénovation.

Les premiers acteurs de l'éducation, les enseignants et les parents, sont surtout préoccupés de la réussite des élèves qu'ils côtoient quotidiennement et voient l'éducation sous l'angle d'une entreprise constituée de personnes œuvrant au niveau de l'école. De leur point de vue, les conditions dans lesquelles se situe leur action sont extrêmement complexes, à cause de l'hétérogénéité qui caractérise maintenant la composition des classes et du rehaussement des exigences en matière de rendement scolaire.

L'éducation au ban des accusés 43

Le jugement

L'éducation primaire et secondaire est le fruit de décisions successives qui ont été prises au fil des années sur les normes, les standards, le niveau de ressources allouées et la répartition des pouvoirs entre le gouvernement, les conseils scolaires et l'école, sans oublier l'opinion publique. Elle est aussi le résultat de l'évolution qu'a connue la société depuis la période d'après-guerre. L'école actuelle reflète les consensus et les conflits qui traversent la société, y compris les affrontements entre le gouvernement et les syndicats.

Le procès de l'école mené par le monde des affaires, les décideurs politiques et les médias, a laissé dans l'ombre des faits importants qui apportent un éclairage différent de la situation.

Depuis le début des années 1990, le taux de participation des jeunes au marché du travail n'a cessé de décroître (Jennings, 1997), mais ce sont effectivement les jeunes les moins scolarisés qui sont les plus susceptibles de se trouver exclus du marché du travail à défaut d'emplois disponibles.

Les entreprises canadiennes participent encore relativement peu à la formation professionnelle des jeunes, contrairement à l'Allemagne, par exemple, même si elles insistent pour que les jeunes possèdent le profil de compétences qu'elles ont défini. Les faiblesses dénoncées passent sous silence toutes les difficultés relatives à l'établissement de données internationales comparables sur les résultats atteints en éducation, et plus particulièrement sur l'abandon scolaire.

Du diagnostic sévère posé par les décideurs politiques découle la rénovation en cours des systèmes scolaires canadiens, de la gouvernance de l'éducation à la réforme du curriculum, sans oublier la formation des maîtres. Ce faisant, on oublie de mentionner que des changements semblables se produisent partout dans le monde occidental et même ailleurs et qu'ils résultent bien plus d'une lame de fond que de circonstances nationales.

Transmettre la culture en même temps que transformer la société est le paradoxe que doit résoudre l'éducation. Il ne faut donc pas s'étonner si la perception de l'éducation primaire et secondaire est toujours un peu éloignée de l'école qu'on souhaiterait avoir.

Le questionnement auquel l'école donne lieu est en quelque sorte étranger à la culture de l'école, une organisation locale pratiquement en situation de monopole, qui rend des services éducatifs à la population de son territoire à partir d'un cadre juridique et réglementaire défini par le conseil scolaire et le gouvernement. Plusieurs écoles sont exemplaires, comme l'a bien montré l'étude de l'Association canadienne d'éducation (Gaskell, 1995). D'autres éprouvent des difficultés de toutes sortes, en particulier celles en milieu socio-économiquement faible, mais pas toutes. Si on considère que les variables lourdes en éducation sont les antécédents socio-économiques des élèves, l'effet que peut avoir le personnel scolaire et l'organisation de l'école sur le destin scolaire de chacun n'est pas négligeable, mais demeure tout de même limité.

L'école est en quelque sorte ballottée entre, d'une part, les politiques qu'elle doit obligatoirement mettre en œuvre, et d'autre part, le contexte socio-économique dans lequel elle est insérée et les ressources qui lui sont allouées, incluant les enseignants. Elle fait partie d'un système sur lequel elle a peu d'influence. Malgré toutes ces contraintes et peut-être à cause d'elles, il y a des écoles qui se démarquent des autres et ce seul fait suffit pour continuer de miser sur l'éducation et d'entretenir l'espoir.

L'éducation, comme l'économie, est en train de s'ajuster au vent de globalisation qui souffle présentement avec force dans les pays occiden-taux. L'éducation s'internationalise et s'adapte progressivement aux normes occidentales, un défi de taille pour un pays comme le Canada où l'éducation relève de la responsabilité des provinces. Ce n'est pas un seul système canadien qui est en train de se transformer mais bien plusieurs.

Ce sont bien plus les enquêtes internationales et les études comparatives menées par des organismes comme l'OCDE qui ont entraîné une réflexion sur le fonctionnement du système éducatif que des facteurs internes. Que le monde des affaires ait aussi sonné l'alarme n'est pas étranger au fait que les entreprises soient très engagées dans les échanges internationaux.

Concernant les débats sur la qualité, les compétences effectivement démontrées par les diplômés du secondaire, il faut pour le moment faire référence aux épreuves internationales alors que le Canada se classe dans la bonne moyenne. Pour des systèmes d'éducation qui ont commencé depuis peu à vérifier l'atteinte des standards, il faut se féliciter de tels résultats.

Sur le plan de l'efficacité, la proportion de diplômés du secondaire pour le groupe d'âge visé, les variations interprovinciales sont inquiétantes. Pour les jeunes, la perception du lien entre éducation et emploi semble moins forte qu'auparavant, bien que la relation entre le niveau de scolarité et l'emploi se vérifie toujours. Le phénomène du raccrochage des jeunes qui retournent aux études après avoir quitté l'école secondaire sans obtenir le diplôme, est également attesté (Frank, 1996), montrant une amélioration des données initiales. Par contre, les élèves des Premières Nations montrent encore des taux de rendement scolaire beaucoup trop faibles. Il est nécessaire de continuer à chercher des solutions pour éviter de marginaliser à vie ceux qui n'auront pas terminé leurs études secondaires.

Quant à l'efficience, la sentence a déjà été prononcée puisque le définancement de l'éducation est bien amorcé.

En conclusion, c'est la société tout entière qui est responsable de l'état de l'éducation et, en dernier recours, ses représentants, les décideurs politiques qui définissent le cadre à l'intérieur duquel le système éducatif devra fonctionner. On le voit clairement par le train de réformes en cours dans les provinces et. de façon accélérée. en Ontario et au Québec. Il y a plusieurs niveaux de transformation d'un système d'éducation susceptibles d'améliorer le taux de réussite des élèves : le préscolaire, le curriculum, les structures scolaires, l'enseignement et l'organisation de l'école, le système d'évaluation. Comme des changements vont se produire dans presque tous ces niveaux pour l'Ontario et dans tous pour le Québec, il faut comprendre que les décideurs politiques ont utilisé tous les moyens à leur disposition pour réorienter l'éducation dans le sens des standards internationaux qui sont en train de s'imposer.

Pour terminer, Bruner (1996), dans un ouvrage récent, associe la culture au mode de gestion de son système éducatif :

«...car l'éducation n'est pas seulement une préparation à l'entrée dans une culture, elle est une des incarnations majeures du mode de vie de cette culture. »

Il ne nous reste plus qu'à faire confiance à la culture canadienne pour l'avenir de l'éducation.

Références

Bruner, Jerome. (1996). *L'éducation, entrée dans la culture* (traduit de l'anglais par Yves Bonin). Paris : Retz.

Cloutier, Richard. (1991). *Les habitudes de vie des élèves du secondaire. Rapport d'étude.* Québec : Ministère de l'Education.

Commission des Etats généraux sur l'éducation. (1996). *Rénover notre système d'éducation : dix chantiers prioritaires.* Québec : Gouvernement du Québec, Ministère de l'éducation.

Commission royale sur l'éducation. (1994). *Pour l'amour d'apprendre. Rapport de la Commission royale sur l'éducation. Une version abrégée.* Toronto : Publications Ontario.

Deslauriers, R.C. (1990). *L'impact des employés analphabètes sur les entreprises canadiennes. Rapport du Centre de perfectionnement des ressources humaines du Conference Board du Canada.* Ottawa : Conference Board du Canada.

Dionne-Proulx, Jacqueline (1995). *Le stress au travail et ses conséquences potentielles à long terme : le cas des enseignants québécois.* Canadian Journal of Education/Revue canadienne d'éducation, 20, 2, 129-145.

Dunning, Paula (1997). *L'éducation au Canada : vue d'ensemble.* Toronto : Association canadienne d'éducation.

Fortin, Laurier et Mercier, Henri. (1994). *Liens entre l'implication des parents à l'école et les comportements de leur enfant en classe du primaire.* Revue des sciences de l'éducation, XX, 3, 529-546.

Frank, Jeffrey. (1996). *Après le secondaire—les premières années.* Ottawa : Statistique Canada et Développement des ressources humaines Canada.

Gaskell, Jane. (1995). *L'école secondaire au Canada. Etude sur les écoles exemplaires.* Toronto : Association canadienne d'éducation.

Hart, Sylvie Ann, Deblois, Claude, Castonguay, Céline. (1994). *L'école secondaire Les Etchemins.* Toronto : Association canadienne d'éducation.

Hrimech, Mohamed et Théoret, Manon. (1997). *L'abandon scolaire au secondaire : une comparaison entre les élèves montréalais nés au Canada et ceux nés à l'étranger.* Canadian Journal of Education/Revue canadienne d'éducation, 22, 3, 268-282.

Jennings, Philip. (1997). *What Explains the Youth Participation Rate ?* Direction générale de la recherche appliquée, Politique stratégique, Développement des ressources humaines Canada. Document de recherche. Ottawa.

Jezak, Monika, Painchaud, Gisèle, d'Anglejan, Alison et Temisjian, Khatoune. (1995). *Le rehaussement des exigences langagières en milieu de travail : l'état de la recherche.* Revue des sciences de l'éducation, XXX1, 2, 371-387.

Lawton, Stephen B. (1996). *Le financement de l'éducation au Canada.* Toronto : Association canadienne d'éducation.

Ministère de l'éducation. (1997). *L'école, tout un programme. Enoncé de politique éducative.* Gouvernement du Québec.

McEwen, Nelly. (1995). *Introduction : Accountability in Education in Canada.* Canadian Journal of Education/Revue canadienne d'éducation, 20, 1, 1-17.

Nagy, Philip. (1996). *International Comparisons of Student Achievement in Mathematics and Science : A Canadian Perspective.* Canadian Journal of Education/Revue canadienne d'éducation, 21, 4, 396-413.

Proulx, Jean-Pierre. (1997). *L'école québécoise, institution et milieu de vie.* Recherches sociographiques, XXXVIII, 2, 221-249.

Saint-Laurent, Lise, Royer, Egide, Hébert, Martine et Tardif, Lyne (1994). *Enquête sur la collaboration famille-école.* Canadian Journal of Education/Revue canadienne d'éducation, 19, 3, 270-286.

Statistics Canada. (1993). *Leaving School—Results From a National Survey Comparing School Leavers and High School Graduates 18 to 20 Years of Age.* Ottawa : Government of Canada.

Statistics Canada. (1996). *Reading the Future: A Portrait of Literacy in Canada. Ottawa : Government of Canada.*

Tremblay, Alain. (1997). *Se dirige-t-on vers un surplus ou une pénurie d'enseignants?* Revue trimestrielle de l'éducation, 4, 1, 53-85.

DAVID F. ROBITAILLE

How Much Do Canadian Students Know about Mathematics and Science?

Abstract

In Canada, as in other countries, there is a great deal of interest in learning how well our schools are preparing students to take their place in society. This interest reflects a growing consensus that a superior educational system and economic productivity are linked. The Third International Mathematics and Science Study (TIMSS) compared the teaching and learning of mathematics and science at the elementary and secondary school levels. The Canadian TIMSS sample was representative of Canada and of five provinces that elected to have their results compared. It included both French- and English-speaking schools. Canadian students performed as well or better than those from the other G-7 countries that participated, with the exception of Japan. A smaller proportion of Canadian students ranked among the highest-scoring students internationally than might be expected. Overall, the results show that Canadian students are doing well in these two important areas of the school curriculum when compared to students in most other countries.

Résumé

Au Canada comme dans d'autres pays, les milieux intéressés souhaitent vivement en savoir davantage sur la façon dont les écoles préparent vraiment leurs élèves à assumer leur place dans la société. Cet intérêt traduit un consensus de plus en plus vaste sur le fait que la productivité économique va de pair avec un système d'éducation supérieur. La Troisième Enquête internationale sur les mathématiques et les sciences (TEIMS) a permis de comparer l'enseignement et l'apprentissage des mathématiques et des sciences aux niveaux primaire et secondaire. L'échantillonnage canadien, composé d'écoles françaises et anglaises, était représentatif du Canada et des cinq provinces qui avaient accepté une comparaison de leurs résultats respectifs. Les élèves canadiens ont affiché des résultats égaux ou supérieurs à ceux de leurs condisciples des autres pays du G-7 qui ont participé à l'étude, exception faite de ceux du Japon. Au plan international, le pourcentage des élèves canadiens qui se sont classés parmi les meilleurs a été inférieur à ce qu'on aurait pu escompter. Dans l'ensemble, les résultats montrent que, par rapport à leurs condisciples dans la plupart des autres pays, les élèves canadiens réussissent bien dans ces deux matières importantes du programme scolaire.

According to a report published by UNESCO last year, there are more than one billion young people—one-fifth of the world's population—attending school, a more than threefold increase in the last 40 years. In virtually every school in the world, a large part of the school day is devoted to the study of mathematics and science, and both subjects are considered to be important parts of most students' programs throughout elementary and secondary school.

In Canada, as in other countries, there is a great deal of interest in how well schools are preparing students to take their place in society. This has a lot to do with mounting public pressure—in Canada and elsewhere—for increased accountability for the large amounts of money devoted to elementary and secondary education. According to a report issued by Statistics Canada and the Council of Ministers of Education (1996), education is the second largest public expenditure in this country, accounting for slightly more than 20 percent of all public expenditures. Of the countries represented in this report, only five spend a greater percentage of their gross national product on elementary and secondary education: Sweden, Norway, Denmark, Iceland, and South Africa.

Canadians are not alone in their concern about students' achievement and the implications of that performance for the future. Governments around the world have shown an interest in assessing what is learned in school, particularly in mathematics and science. This reflects a growing consensus that scientific literacy and economic productivity are tightly linked. It is now widely believed that the failure of a nation to educate its work force threatens that nation's ability to keep pace economically in the international marketplace. It has, therefore, become very important for nations to know more about the performance of their school systems.

International Comparisons in Education

Valid international comparisons across systems of education are difficult to make because of the numbers of variables involved, because of the lack of sophisticated ways of accounting for the influence of many of those variables, and because of the fact that some of the variables involved are beyond the control of the educational system. Torsten Husén, an eminent Swedish educator, once referred to international comparative studies in education as exercises in comparing the incomparable.

In making that statement, Professor Husén was not intending to imply that international comparisons and international studies were pointless. On the contrary, he was saying that international studies were important precisely because the comparisons were so difficult to make. Educational systems, as products of particular cultures, are very different from one another in a number of fundamental ways; one needs to guard against the temptation to make oversimplified generalizations or comparisons. There is a danger that invalid comparisons will be made or inappropriate conclusions arrived at. However, comparisons based on valid, reliable, and accurate data have a greater likelihood of providing useful information for policy makers than comparisons based on no data or on ill-informed opinion.

The Third International Mathematics and Science Study (TIMSS) is the largest and most ambitious study conducted to date under the auspices of the International Association for the Evaluation of Educational Achievement (IEA). The overall purpose of the study was to compare the teaching and learning of mathematics and science at the elementary and secondary school levels with the aim of informing educators around the world about exemplary practices and outcomes.

IEA, the Organization

IEA is an association of associations; its members are universities, research institutes and ministries of education. The primary goals of the organization are to conduct co-operative international research studies in education and to contribute to the development of educational research expertise around the world. IEA is chartered in Belgium and its headquarters are located in Amsterdam. In the past 35 years IEA has carried out numerous international studies and now has over 50 members. Most of the member organizations are national in scope, but there are several exceptions. For example, Belgium is represented by two separate members: one representing the French-speaking part of the country, and the other representing the Flemish-speaking part. Scotland has its own representation, as did three Canadian provinces until earlier this year: British Columbia, Ontario, and Québec. Canadian membership in IEA is now housed in the secretariat of the Council of Ministers of Education.

Structure of the Study

TIMSS focused on three populations of students. Population 1 consisted of all students enrolled in the pair of adjacent grades or levels that included most nine-year olds: Grades 3 and 4 in Canada, and in most other countries. Population 2 included all students in the pair of adjacent grades or levels with the largest proportion of thirteen-year olds: Grades 7 and 8 in most countries. Population 3 included all students in the last year of secondary education, regardless of program.

Of the three, Population 3 was the most difficult to specify, and the results at that level will be the most difficult to interpret appropriately because of the wide variety of programs available in different countries at the senior secondary level as well as the existence, in some countries, of major exit points from the school system at several age or grade levels. In Canada, the Population 3 sample included students enrolled in Grade 12 in most parts of the country, students registered in OAC courses in Ontario, and students enrolled in CEGEPs in Québec.

Over 50 countries participated in one or more TIMSS-related activities over the course of the project. Of these, 41 collected student achievement data for Population 2; 26, for Population 1; and about 20 for Population 3. Canadian and international reports have been published for Populations 1 and 2, and the Population 3 report will be published in February, 1998. A list of the countries that participated in Populations 1 and 2 is shown in Table 1.

In order to ensure the quality of the data collected for the study, participants were required to observe strict quality-control guidelines on every aspect of the study, including sampling of schools and classrooms, translation of instruments, and training of coders and markers. The guidelines called for countries to select nationally representative samples of schools, both public and non-public. The goal was to have 85 percent of the schools contacted agree to participate and for 85 percent of the students registered in the classes selected from those schools to participate.

About half the participants, including Canada, met all of the sampling requirements. Of the remainder, a number either had to use replacement schools to reach the 85 percent level, or did not include all eligible students in the sample-selection process: e.g., Latvia included only Latvian-speaking schools. Those countries are identified in the table by an asterisk. A number of other countries failed to meet one or more of the sampling guidelines, and some caution should be exercised in interpreting their results since they might be biased in some way. Those countries are identified by two asterisks.

The national centre in each country did whatever was possible to meet the sampling requirements of the study, but not all were able to meet the strict criteria that had been agreed upon. In several cases, national centres encountered resistance from schools or teachers, and so failed to meet the 85 percent school participation criterion. This was the case in Australia, Austria, Belgium (French), Bulgaria, the Netherlands, and Scotland. Four countries—Colombia, Germany, Romania, and Slovenia—elected to test in grades other than the ones internationally agreed upon in order to get a better curriculum match, even though those grades did not contain the largest proportions of age cohorts being studied. The students selected in those instances were, on the average, somewhat older than those selected in other countries. More complete information on sampling procedures and outcomes is provided in the quality control report of the study (Martin & Mullis, 1996).

Table 1: Countries participating in TIMSS, Populations 1 and 2

◆ Australia**	◆ Korea, Republic of
◆ Austria**	◆ Kuwait**
Belgium(Flemish)*	◆ Latvia (LSS)*
Belgium (French)**	Lithuania*
Bulgaria	◆ Netherlands**
◆ Canada	◆ New Zealand
Columbia**	◆ Norway
◆ Cyprus	◆ Portugal
◆ Czech Republic	Romania**
Denmark	Russian Federation
◆ England*	◆ Scotland**
France	◆ Singapore
Germany**	Slovak Republic
◆ Greece**	◆ Slovenia**
◆ Hong Kong	South Africa**
◆ Hungary	Spain
◆ Iceland	Sweden
◆ Iran	Switzerland*
◆ Ireland	◆ Thailand**
◆ Israel**	◆ United States*
◆ Japan	

◆*Participated in Population 1.*   **Replacement schools used*   ***Did not meet all of the sampling requirements*

Contextual Data about the Participating Countries

It is well known that a number of sociological factors, including socio-economic status and parental support for schools, have an important influence on how well students perform in school. It is also well known that schools cannot do a great deal to compensate for the influence of some of these variables, or can do so only in exceptional circumstances given appropriate levels of support. The fact that a particular approach to teaching or curriculum works well in Country A, is no guarantee that the same approach will work well in Country B.

David F. Robitaille

Table 2: Selected demographic characteristics of TIMSS Countries

	Pop. (1000's)	Net Enr %	Educ % GNP	# Computers	Sch Year	Hrs/ Week	Pds/ Week	Period Lgth	Same Course	Tch/ Wk
Australia	17 617	98	3.69	68	197	26	32	47	65	27
Austria	7 863	90	4.24	17	214	30	34	50	29	21
Belgium	10 046	95	3.70	16	182	28	32	50	100	23
Bulgaria	8 870	82	3.06	8	164	32	32	45	100	28
Canada	28 817	98	4.62	44	186	26	32	51	84	27
Colombia	33 986	85	2.83	9	180	32	34	44	97	28
Cyprus	726	97	3.60	2	172	26	35	45	100	21
Czech Rep.	10 296		3.75	9	199	24	30	45	90	22
Denmark	5 165	98	4.80	26	200	29	29	45	99	
England	57 924	96	3.57	80	190	25	33	47	34	22
France	57 508	99	3.61	21	173	30	29	55	76	19
Germany	80 857	81	2.43	13	196	25	31	45	74	23
Greece	10 377	94	2.27	6	167	30	32	44	100	19
Hong Kong	5 809		1.34	28	172	32	47	39	100	35
Hungary	10 210	92	4.31	11	182	28				30
Iceland	263		4.77	16	160	24	34	41	77	31
Iran	64 169	97	3.93	0	209	33	33	60	96	29
Ireland	3 524	90	4.21	18	168	28	42	40	24	31
Israel	5 254		3.72	42	209	37	35	49	63	23
Japan	124 536	100	2.82	23	231	30			99	19
Korea, Rep.	44 131	100	3.43	25	211	35	36	45	100	20
Kuwait	1 775		3.46	24						15
Latvia	2 611	81	2.85	9	175	33	34	40	97	26
Lithuania	3 712		2.18	6	191	29	31	45	87	25
Netherlands	15 285	94	3.30	39	196	32	32	49	30	25
New Zealand	3 485	99	3.15	57	190	26	26	57	61	24
Norway	4 299	99	5.26	5						22
Philippines	64 800		1.78							
Portugal	9 838	100	2.98	8	182	32	32	50	98	23
Romania	23 023	77	1.89	1	175	32	32	49	98	16
Russian Fed.	147 760	96		11	193	27	32	42	90	25
Scotland	5132		3.57	109	192	28	33	51	72	29
Singapore	2 793	100	3.38	68	200	25	43	35	20	40
Slovak Rep.	5 314		2.69	6	195	31	31	45	82	24
Slovenia	1 937		4.20	8	180	28	28	45	89	24
South Africa	39 659	92	5.12							
Spain	39 514	100	3.17	6	181	26	25	57	100	23
Sweden	8 694	99	4.92	26	181	35	31	47	42	24
Switzerland	7 056	94	3.72	16	234	29	33	46	63	26
Thailand	57 585		3.00	8	199	38	37	50	83	20
United States	257 925	100	4.02	15	179	30	35	50	17	32

Net Enr: percent of children at the age of the first year of compulsory education that are actually in school; Educ %GDP: Amount spent on education as a percent of GNP; # Computers: Average number of computers per school*; Sch Year: Number of teaching days per year*; Hrs/Week, Pds/Week, Period Lgth: Average number of hours of instruction per week, and the division of those hours into periods*; Same course: percent of schools reporting that all Population 2 students take the same mathematics course; Tch/Wk: Hours of instruction per week as reported on TIMSS survey.

Table 2 presents information about a number of demographic characteristics of the countries participating in TIMSS. No claim is made that these
are the most important characteristics to be considered in trying to interpret
the results of the study; they are nothing more or nothing less than a selection of variables which provide additional information about the participating countries that may be useful in trying to interpret the results. Another
TIMSS publication (Robitaille, 1997), the so-called *TIMSS Encyclopedia,*
provides a much more comprehensive discussion of a number of topics
closely related to the teaching and learning of mathematics and science.

The table shows a variety of different kinds of data about the participating countries, their schools and their teachers. The first three columns summarize some basic demographic data about the countries. For example, the
third column shows, as was mentioned earlier, that Canada spends a greater
proportion of its gross national product on education that any of these
countries except Sweden, Norway, Denmark, Iceland, and South Africa.

The fourth column shows the number of computers that participating
schools reported were available to Population 2 students and teachers for
instructional purposes in the spring of 1995. Responses ranged from none
at all to a high of 109 in Scotland, and the median was 15. Canadian schools
reported an average of 44 computers per school, putting them among the
countries with the largest numbers of computers available for instructional
purposes. Unfortunately, it appears that those computers are not used very
frequently for teaching either mathematics or science.

The average length of the school year reported by school principals in
these countries is almost 190 days long; and the Canadian result, at 186
days on the average, is very close to the international mean. Japan and
Switzerland reported much longer school years.

Canadian school principals report that Grade 8 classes are in session
for an average of 27 instructional hours per week. This is higher than the international average, which is about 24 hours per week. Data from teachers
show that class sizes in Canada are relatively large, so the overall impression is that Canadian teachers have heavier teaching loads than teachers in
many other comparable countries.

The second last column in the table indicates the percentage of schools
which reported that all of their Grade 8 students took the same course in
mathematics. Countries with a low percent in this column offer two or
more mathematics courses at this level, and students are directed by some
means into one or the other of those courses. Thus, in the United States, less
than 20 percent of the schools reported that all of their students took the
same mathematics course; it is well known that there are several different
programs in mathematics available to Grade 8 students in that country.

Several countries, including four countries with very high achievement on the TIMSS test, reported that all of their students took the same course at this level. Canada, at 84 percent, is among the countries least likely to separate students into different mathematics programs at this age level.

The Canadian sample for Population 2 included slightly more than 17,000 students evenly divided between Grades 7 and 8. This was by far the largest sample of students drawn by any country participating in the study, the large size being required to produce stable estimates of results at the provincial level. All of the data collection instruments for the study, including questionnaires and test booklets, were produced in both French and English.

Tables 3 and 4 summarize results from several items on the questionnaire administered to students at the time of testing. The items focus on a number of demographic characteristics of the Canadian samples.

Table 3: Characteristics of the Canadian Population 2 Student Sample %

	Canada	AB	BC	NB	NF	ON	Int'l*
Born in Canada	90	92	85	97	98	90	94
Speak language of test at home	90	92	86	97	97	74	85
Live with mother	94	93	94	94	95	94	89
Live with father	75	74	71	75	81	78	88
Mother born in Canada	77	80	64	94	98	73	89
Father born in Canada	74	78	60	93	98	69	88

* refers to students' respective countries

Almost all Grade 8 students in Canada, 90 percent of them, were born in Canada, and they speak either English or French at home always or almost always. British Columbia, at 83 percent, had the lowest proportion of Canadian-born students and the second lowest proportion of students reporting that they spoke either English or French at home almost always. Ontario students reported the lowest proportion on this language-spoken-at-home variable, at 74 percent. This result is largely due to the fact that only 47 percent of the Franco-Ontarian student sample said that they spoke French at home almost all the time. An additional 36 percent indicated that they spoke French at home some of the time.

About three-quarters of Grade 8 students live at home with both of their parents, and the same proportion of students say that both their parents were born in Canada. There are quite significant differences across provinces insofar as the latter variable is concerned. Over 90 percent of students in New Brunswick and Newfoundland say that both their parents were born in Canada. Those proportions are considerably lower in three other provinces, and especially in British Columbia. Only about 60 percent of British Columbia students reported that both their parents were born in Canada.

Almost all Grade 4 students in Canada, 93 percent of them, were born in Canada, and they speak either English or French at home always or almost always. Ontario, at 89 percent, had the lowest proportion of Canadian-born students as well as the lowest proportion of students reporting that they spoke either English or French at home almost always, at 79 percent. The low proportion reported for the language-spoken-at-home variable is largely due to the fact that only 38 percent of the Franco-Ontarian student sample said that they spoke French at home almost all of the time. An additional 51 percent indicated that they spoke French at home some of the time.

Table 4: Characteristics of the Canadian Population 1 Student Sample %						
	Canada	AB	BC	NB	NF	ON
Born in Canada	93	93	93	96	97	89
Speak language of test at home	86	87	91	91	92	79
Live with mother	95	94	93	94	95	94
Live with father	76	73	73	76	79	77
Mother born in Canada	78	76	75	90	95	66
Father born in Canada	75	75	74	90	94	60

Over 90 percent of Grade 4 students live at home with their mother, and 76 percent live with their father. About three-quarters of students reported that both their parents were born in Canada, but there are quite significant differences across provinces insofar as the latter variable is concerned. Over 90 percent of students in New Brunswick and Newfoundland said that both their parents were born in Canada. These proportions are considerably lower in three other provinces, and especially in Ontario. Only about 60 percent of Ontario students reported that both their parents were born in Canada.

Data Sources

It is estimated that about 500,000 students in more than 15,000 schools in over 40 countries—along with their mathematics teachers, science teachers, and principals—participated in TIMSS. Students responded to a questionnaire which sought information about their opinions, attitudes, and interests as well as to achievement items in both mathematics and science. Teachers completed questionnaires dealing with their academic and professional preparation, the instructional approaches they used, and the content they taught. Principals provided information about their schools, the students, and the teachers.

The achievement items used to evaluate what students knew and were able to do in mathematics and science were assembled through a consensus-building process designed to obtain agreement from participating countries about what should be tested and how. As would be expected in any large-scale evaluation study, the final item pool included many multiple-choice items; however, it also included a large number of both short-answer and extended-response items. The achievement testing was done as late as possible in the school year in order to enhance comparability across countries.

All of the test items—in fact, all of the instruments used in the study—were developed in English, with the English version serving as the standard. They were translated by the participants into 30 other languages, using a process of two or more parallel translations followed by an adjudication to resolve any differences. Final translations were verified and approved centrally.

No student responded to all of the achievement items. The items were distributed among eight booklets, each requiring about 90 minutes to complete, and each student was issued one booklet. Students were not permitted to use calculators during the testing.

Canadian Participation in TIMSS

In Canada, unlike most other countries, there is no federal ministry of education. Each province and territory has exclusive jurisdiction over elementary and secondary education within its boundaries, and efforts by the federal government to influence educational policy or to provide targeted funding for education have traditionally been resisted by one or more provinces. There are a number of other countries where each state or province has jurisdiction over its own educational system; Australia, Germany, and the United States are good examples of such systems. However, in each of these cases the federal government plays a major role in funding or policy making for the system as a whole.

Getting all of the provinces and territories to agree to participate in a common activity in the educational domain is a non-trivial task, since provincial agendas and priorities for education vary from jurisdiction to jurisdiction and since there is no governmental organization whose mandate it is to set such agendas or priorities. The Council of Ministers of Education is an organization that provides a forum for the ministers of education and their officials to discuss matters of common concern, but even the Council cannot guarantee that all of the provinces will participate in the programs which it supports. The School Achievement Indicators Program is a case in point.

Canadian participation in TIMSS was unique because every province and territory agreed to participate, at least initially. That is, they all agreed, at a minimum, to have their schools and students included in the nationally representative sample that was selected by Statistics Canada. Regrettably, shortly before the student testing was carried out in the spring of 1995, the newly appointed minister and deputy minister of education in Prince Edward Island rescinded the decision that had been taken by their predecessors to have schools and students from that province represented in the study. Fortunately, given the size of the population of students in PEI, this involved very few schools, not enough to affect the results in any meaningful way.

Because of the way education is organized in Canada, it was clear that there would be a great deal of interest in how things such as students' achievement, teaching practices, and curriculum varied within the country among provinces and territories. In fact, provincial-level results may well be of more interest in this country than national ones. For that reason, every effort was made to encourage as many provinces as possible to select samples large enough to provide good estimates of all of the results at the provincial level as well as contributing to the national results. In the end, five provinces—Newfoundland, New Brunswick, Ontario, Alberta, and British Columbia—chose to participate in this way, although the New Brunswick sample included English-speaking schools only. This means that, in addition to comparing the performance of Canadian students to those in other countries, it is possible to make inter-provincial comparisons among those five provinces and for those provinces to compare themselves with any of the other countries participating in the study. Characteristics of the Canadian samples for Populations 1 and 2 are summarized in Tables 5 and 6.

Table 5: Characteristics of the Canadian School Sample, Population 2			
	Schools Selected	Schools Participating	Students Tested	Participation Rate
CANADA	414	379	17 188	95 %
Alberta	55	51	2 241	92 %
British Columbia	29	26	784	99 %
Manitoba	6	3	147	101 %
New Brunswick	30	20	945	90 %
Newfoundland	40	391	733	102 %
Northwest Territories	4	4	163	102 %
Nova Scotia	5	2	105	64 %
Ontario	189	189	5 594	95 %
Prince Edward Island	4	0	0	0 %
Quebec	42	38	2 205	97 %
Saskatchewan	6	3	156	57 %
Yukon	4	4	147	101 %

The sample was drawn so as to be representative of Canada and of the five provinces that elected to have their results compared. Schools were randomly selected proportional to size within each province or territory from a list of all schools, both public and non-public. The sample included both French-speaking and English-speaking schools.

The International Coordinating Centre for TIMSS and the National Centre for TIMSS-Canada were housed in the Faculty of Education at the University of British Columbia. Funding for international coordination and for carrying out the study in Canada was provided through a grant from Human Resources Development, Canada and contributions from the over-sampling provinces.

All of the instruments for the study were translated into French, and a process was set up to finalize the translations and settle any differences between the translations that were done in Québec and those done in Ontario. Coding of the open-ended items was done in British Columbia for all of the English-language responses, and in Ontario for all the French-language ones.

Table 6: Characteristics of the Canadian School Sample, Population 1

	Schools Selected	Schools Participating	Students Tested	Participation Rate
CANADA	412	379	16,142	90 %
Alberta	55	50	2017	91 %
British Columbia	19	18	662	95 %
Manitoba	6	3	124	50 %
New Brunswick	22	20	886	91 %
Newfoundland	50	48	1954	96 %
Northwest Territories	4	3	151	75 %
Nova Scotia	5	3	118	60 %
Ontario	200	195	8470	98 %
Prince Edward Island	4	0	0	0 %
Quebec	37	32	1490	85 %
Saskatchewan	6	3	136	42 %
Yukon	4	4	134	100 %

Achievement Results

About 35,000 students in over 750 Canadian schools participated in the TIMSS survey at the Populations 1 and 2 levels. Each student was given 90 minutes to complete a background questionnaire and a set of science and mathematics achievement items. The achievement items for each population were distributed among eight booklets, each containing both mathematics and science items. The items were of three types: multiple choice, short answer, and extended response.

In the sections that follow, the performance of Canadian students on the achievement survey is summarized by grade level and by subject. This is followed by a brief discussion of some of the major implications of these findings.

Population 2 (Grade 8)

There was considerable variability across countries on both the mathematics and the science tests, with mean percent correct scores ranging from a low of 24 percent to a high of 79 percent. Students from the following countries outperformed Canadian students in both mathematics and science at this level: Austria, Czech Republic, Japan, Korea, and Singapore.

Grade 8 students in Canada had a mean percent correct score of 59 in mathematics, significantly higher than the international mean and as good as or better than the mean scores in 30 of the 40 other countries participating in the study. The scores of Canadian students were significantly higher than the international average in four content areas: fractions and number sense; geometry; data representation, analysis, and probability; and proportionality. Canadian results were not significantly different from the international mean in the other two areas, algebra and measurement.

In science, Canadian Grade 8 students did as well as or better than students from 31 other countries, attaining a mean percent correct score of 59. They attained scores higher than the international average in four of the five science content areas: earth science, life science, physics, and environment and the nature of science. In chemistry, the Canadian result was the same as the international average.

Population 1 (Grade 4)

The achievement of Canadian Grade 4 students was higher than the international mean in both mathematics and science: slightly above in mathematics and significantly above in science. Only Korea, Japan, and the Netherlands outperformed Canadian students in both subject areas at this level.

Grade 4 students in Canada attained an average score of 60 in mathematics, which was as good as or better than the scores in 17 of the 26 Population 1 countries. Canadian scores were better than the international average in four content areas: whole numbers; data representation, analysis, and probability; geometry; and patterns, relations, and functions. Their scores were lower in two areas: fractions and proportionality; and measurement, estimation, and number sense.

In science, Canadian Grade 4 students attained a score of 64 percent, 5 percentage points higher than the international mean. This score was as good as or better than that of 20 countries. In all content areas, Canadian scores were significantly higher than the international average.

Top-scoring Students in Mathematics

How good are our best students and how do they compare to their counterparts in other countries? Figure 1 shows, for 14 of the Population 2 countries, what proportion of the country's Grade 8 students placed among the top 10 percent of all the students who wrote the TIMSS Population 2 mathematics test, what proportion placed among the top 25 percent, and what proportion placed among the top 50 percent.

The graph shows that, in Singapore, 45 percent of Grade 8 students were in the top 10 percent internationally; 75 percent, in the top quarter, and 95 percent in the top half. In Canada, on the other hand, only seven percent of Grade 8 students were in the top tenth, 25 percent in the top quarter, and 60 percent in the top half internationally.

If we were to select a random sample of 100 students from among those who scored in the top 10 percent on the TIMSS test, the analysis says that 12 of them would likely come from Singapore, nine each from Korea and Japan, seven from Hong Kong, two each from England, France, and Germany, and one from the United States. Two of them would be Canadian.

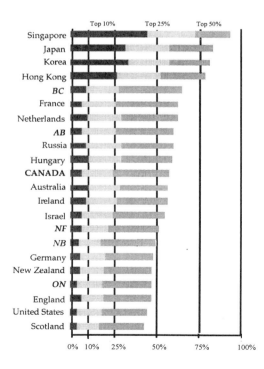

Figure 1: Performance of top Grade 8 students from selected countries.

Figure 2 shows the same kind of information at the Grade 4 level. Forty percent of Grade 4 students from Singapore who wrote the TIMSS tests scored in the top 10 percent of students internationally, 60 percent were in the top 25 percent, and more than 80 percent were in the top half. Results for Canada show that 7 percent were in the top 10 percent internationally; about 20 percent, in the top quarter; and 50 percent, in the top half.

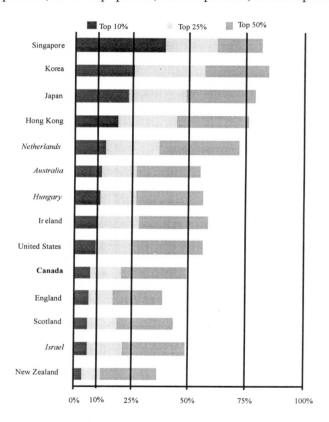

Figure 2: Performance of top Grade 4 students from selected countries.

Gender Differences

Canadian girls and boys performed equally well in mathematics and science in both grade levels. This represents a significant change over the past 20 years. Both girls and boys in Grade 8 attained a mean of 59 percent correct in mathematics. In science, boys obtained an overall mean score of 60 percent and girls 58 percent, a difference that is not statistically significant. Similar findings were reported in most other countries.

Discussion

The performance of Canadian students on the TIMSS achievement survey was significantly better than the international average across all participating countries for science in both Grade 4 and Grade 8, and for mathematics in Grade 8. In the case of Grade 4 mathematics, the Canadian average was not significantly different from the international average. Students in Japan and Korea consistently outperformed Canadian students at both population levels. Canadian students did as well as or better than those from any of the other G-7 countries that participated, with the exception of Japan.

Five Canadian provinces—British Columbia, Alberta, Ontario, New Brunswick (English-speaking schools), and Newfoundland—selected large enough samples for their results to be reported independently. In general, scores from British Columbia and Alberta were highest, while scores from Ontario and New Brunswick were substantially lower. Scores from Alberta were consistently among the highest from any jurisdiction at both grade levels and in both subject areas.

These results demonstrate that Canadian students are learning a great deal of mathematics and science, and that their performance compares favourably with that of students in other countries. They also show that, in Canada and most other countries, boys and girls are achieving at similar levels, a significant change from 20 years ago when gender differences in mathematics and science achievement at these age and grade levels were prevalent.

On the other hand, the results point to areas where improvement is needed, and prominent among these is the performance of our best students. A smaller proportion of Canadian students ranks among the highest-scoring students internationally than might be expected on the basis of our overall standing. This may mean that we are not doing enough to identify, encourage, and channel our very best students, while other countries seem to be doing a much better job of this.

Are Canadian students doing well enough; and, if not, what should we be doing? We already spend more money per capita on K—12 education than almost all other countries. Our teachers are well educated. We compare favourably with most of our economic competitors on variables such as class size, hours of instruction, and length of the school year.

Contributing to the fact of higher costs for education in this country than in most other jurisdictions are factors such as the decentralized nature of educational governance and the concomitant duplication of administration and service costs, the distribution of our population and the costs associated with small schools and transportation, partial or full public funding for independent schools, parallel French and English school systems in most provinces, and equalization of educational opportunity for all students. Would we be willing to abandon any of these goals, and what difference would it make if we did?

Data from TIMSS, as well as from other studies, shows that there are a number of societal and personal variables that might be worth examining in this connection. In the Asian countries that participated in TIMSS, there seems to be a much greater degree of parental interest and involvement in school matters. Many students in those countries attend out-of-school, privately funded "learning centres," where they are given additional practice particularly on computational skills. There is also considerable pressure on students to succeed in order to be accepted into the more prestigious schools at the next higher level.

Of course there are educationally relevant differences as well, and some TIMSS-related research is producing interesting findings in those areas. Videotapes were made of approximately 100 Grade 8 mathematics classrooms in Germany, Japan, and the United States by trained videographers, and those tapes are now available for comparative analysis. Preliminary results indicate that that there are important differences in the ways lessons are structured in the three countries, in the level of sophistication of the mathematical content being taught, and in the kinds of tasks students are called upon to perform. Unfortunately no such data are available for Canadian classrooms.

Future Activities

To date, TIMSS has produced international reports for Populations 1 and 2, and a separate report dealing with the "hands-on" problem-solving component of the study. The Population 3 report is scheduled for release in late February 1998, and it will deal with the mathematical and scientific literacy of students completing secondary school, regardless of the kind of program they are enrolled in, as well as the achievement of students who have specialized in either mathematics or physics. Publication of the Population 3 report will bring the first phase of the study to an end.

The first round of TIMSS reports has barely scratched the surface of the analytic potential of the data, and efforts are under way to secure funds to make it possible to carry out more in-depth, secondary analyses of the results in order to increase the potential impact of the study on Canadian education. A lot of money has already been spent to collect the data, and a lot of valuable time has been donated to the project by students, teachers, administrators, and researchers. It would be unfortunate indeed if we did not make a real effort to use this resource to work toward the improvement of our educational system.

A follow-up study, TIMSS—R, or the TIMSS Repeat study, is scheduled to be carried out in 1999 with significant financial support from the US National Center for Education Statistics and the National Science Foundation. There is considerable interest among several of the provinces that participated in TIMSS, as well as in the Council of Ministers of Education, in participating in the repeat study. It will provide data for trend analyses and for cohort studies since the Population 1 and 2 students in the first round will, in 1999, be in Populations 2 and 3, respectively.

References

Martin, M. and Mullis, I. (Eds.) (1996). *Third International Mathematics and Science Study: Quality Assurance in Data Collection.* Boston: Boston College.

Robitaille, D. F. (Ed.) (1997). *National Contexts for Mathematics and Science Education: An Encyclopedia of the Educational Systems Participating in TIMSS.* Vancouver: Pacific Educational Press.

Robitaille, D. F., Taylor, A. R., and Orpwood, G. (1996). *The TIMSS-Canada Report. Volume 1: Grade 8.* Vancouver: Department of Curriculum Studies, UBC.

Robitaille, D. F., Taylor, A. R., and Orpwood, G. (1997). *The TIMSS-Canada Report. Volume 2: Grade 4.* Vancouver: Department of Curriculum Studies, UBC.

Robitaille, D. F., Taylor, A. R., Brigden, S. R., and Marshall, M. A. (1997). *The TIMSS-Canada Report. Volume 3: Hands-on Problem Solving.* Vancouver: Department of Curriculum Studies, UBC.

Statistics Canada and Council of Ministers of Education, Canada. (1996). *A Statistical Portrait of Elementary and Secondary Education in Canada.* Ottawa: Canadian Education Statistics Council.

GILLES PAQUET, MSRC

Canada as a Disconcerted Learning Economy: A Governance Challenge

Abstract

The Canadian socio-economy is a complex adaptive system supposedly endowed with good co-ordination and governance since the United Nations have suggested that Canada has the best quality of life in the world. Yet, a look at Canada's performance through the lenses of the standard measures of economic performance (real GDP per capita growth, productivity growth) or through more comprehensive indicators (Measure of Economic Welfare, Genuine Progress Indicator) or via social indicators (Index of Social Health) would appear to paint a much less flattering picture. The paper suggests that this is because the Canadian socio-economy suffers from disconcertion: there is a disconnection between its governance and its circumstances. To support this diagnosis, the paper explores the dynamics of the learning economy and points to evidence that Canadian institutions currently in place tend not to promote effective learning. This poses a governance challenge and the paper explores four strategies deserving consideration as ways to repair the governance system: overcoming Canada's national adversarial systems, a dramatic broadening of the notion of learning and competence in the new world of work, supporting the local systems of innovation, and developing a notion of organizational citizenship as a move toward stakeholder capitalism and better macro-social learning.

Résumé

La socio-économie canadienne est un système complexe en adaptation continue dont la co-ordination et la gouvernance sont présumément en bon état puisque les Nations Unies ont suggéré que le Canada a la meilleure qualité de vie au monde. Mais un coup d'œil à la performance du Canada à l'aune des mesures traditionnelles de performance économique (croissance du PIB réel per capita, croissance de la productivité) ou d'indicateurs plus compréhensifs (mesure de bien-être économique, indicateur de vrai progrès) ou d'indicateurs sociaux (indice de santé sociale) semble suggérer un portrait moins flatteur du Canada. Ce mémoire suggère que c'est parce que la socio-économie canadienne est déconcertée : il y a déconnection entre sa trame et sa gouvernance. Pour appuyer ce diagnostic, le texte explore la dynamique de l'économie en apprentissage et montre que les institutions canadiennes en place ne promeuvent pas un apprentissage efficace. Voilà qui pose un défi à la gouvernance et le mémoire explore quatre stratégies qui méritent notre attention au moment de procéder aux réparations du système de gouvernance : surmonter les tensions engendrées par les systèmes adversaires au Canada, élargir dramatiquement la notion d'apprentissage et de compétences dans le nouveau monde du travail, supporter les systèmes locaux d'innovation, et développer la notion de citoyenneté organisationnelle comme stratégie de passage à un capitalisme nouveau et un meilleur apprentissage macro-social.

"The refusal to admit achievement is achievement in itself"
                                                    Bruce Hutchison

Introduction

It having been established at the 1996 symposium of the Royal Society of
Canada that Canada was not legally dead, and might even survive into the
next century as a socio-political economy, the 1997 symposium proposes
to develop a clinical diagnosis of the state of well-being of Canada in terms
of various vital signs. In a clinical context, vague references to vital signs
cannot suffice, nor can idle debates about possible illnesses, nor vaticina-
tions about putative pharmakons. A reasonably sound appreciation of the
state of the patient is essential, precise hypotheses about the nature and
source of the malaise must be formulated and validated, and promising
strategies must be sketched to ensure that, at the very least, the worst possible outcomes are made as unlikely as possible.

When applied to the Canadian economy, these imperatives are more
easily decreed than realized. For the Canadian economy is a complex adaptive system. Millions of active agents are interacting in complex ways (either directly or through all sorts of networks, organizations, subsystems or
institutions), and adapting continually to new circumstances, and to each
other, in creative ways, within an overall system that maintains some degree of coherence and persistence.

The Canadian socio-economy is akin to other complex adaptive systems (like our central nervous system or our immune system or our ecosystem). For instance, our immune system is a brigade of antibodies that continually fight and destroy an ever-changing cast of invading bacteria and
viruses of such a variety that it must continually learn, adapt, improvise and
overcome for us to survive. Our central nervous system is a coalition of
hundreds of millions of neurons interacting, combining and recombining in
different patterns, as it deals with a complex and ever-changing context,
and yields an always renewed ability to cope, to anticipate, to adapt and to
learn (Holland 1995). In complex adaptive systems, the whole is not the

*I am grateful to Jeffrey Roy and Chris Wilson for their comments and help,
and to Hans Messinger, Satya Brink and Allen Zeesman for the data and
analyses they have made available to me. None of these persons should be
regarded as guilty by association for the use I have made of their data,
analyses, and comments. The assistance of Anne Burgess is gratefully
acknowledged.*

simple sum of the behaviours of the part: it is an aggregate of diverse elements, *in interaction in all sorts of ways*, that are continually developing networks and subsystems, self-reinforcing mechanisms, and a capacity to learn and to adapt through these devices.

The multiplicity of ways in which evolution may materialize explains why even the rigidly programmed behaviour of individual ants does not prevent the ant nest from being highly adaptive in the face of a variety of hazards. Evolution, in such a case, materializes through "aggregate interactions": what cannot be accomplished by the individual is realized by internal and external structures that are quite separate from the competencies of the individual. As Holland puts it, "it is much like an intelligent organism constructed of relatively unintelligent parts" (Holland 1995:11). The same may be said of our central nervous system, of our immune system, of our large cities, or of our socio-economies.

Inquiring about the economic well-being of Canada is attempting to gauge the extent to which Canadians have succeeded in organizing and instituting their political socio-economy, and in governing themselves, in ways that have had a high yield in economic and socio-political terms, and promise to continue to do so. It is an effort to develop, on the basis of aggregate measurements of performance, a diagnosis of the coordination and governance of the Canadian political socio-economy.

Coordination is effected through the rules of the Canadian socio-economic-political game, its organizational and institutional orders. At any time, these rules may be regarded as imperfect, but more or less viable sets of armistices that have evolved between the geo-technical context and the values and plans of the stakeholders in Canada and elsewhere.

Governance is about guiding. It is the process through which an organization steers itself through time, and its evolution is elicited. This is the result of both an ongoing adaptation-adoption process between the organization and its environment, and of interventions by different stakeholders, through the use of different levers, in an effort to modify the speed and the direction of the learning process in ways that favour them.

Coordination and governance may take many forms and shapes. The socio-economy may be structured in hierarchical ways and steered by some central authority as in a warship or in a planned economy; the stewardship may also be generally decentralized and distributed, and operate through subtle interactive adjustments, as in a sailing ship, or through the "invisible hand" of the market mechanism. In most modern societies, coordination and governance are a mixture of these diverse mechanisms—some based on top-down coercion, others on horizontal exchange relations or on relationships based on solidarity, and still others on bottom-up self-organizing processes generating a sense of direction from below.

The main thrust of this paper is to establish that, despite the celebration of our achievements by our political leaders, there are serious reasons to believe that the situation is not as rosy as is usually argued: the process of coordination and governance of the Canadian system is in bad shape and in need of serious repair.

In the next section, I examine the evolution of a number of rough indicators, and suggest that they raise concerns about the performance of the Canadian economy. Many paradoxes emerge from the patterns of change in the indicators in use. In the following section, I examine the dynamics of the new knowledge-based learning economy, and show how its performance has come to depend more and more on its coordination and governance mechanisms, on its *capacity to transform,* its *capacity to learn.* In the final sections, I suggest some reasons why the Canadian governance system would appear to suffer from learning disabilities, and I explain why this is responsible for its lacklustre economic performance; I then explore the main repairs that may be required in the Canadian coordination and governance system if the Canadian socio-economy's performance is to significantly improve.

The Paradoxes of Canada's Performance

Canadians and their political leaders have unabashedly celebrated the gold medal that Canada received from the United Nations as the country endowed with the best quality of life in the world. Nobody bothered to examine critically either the salmagundi of benchmarks on which this global indicator of quality of life was built, or what it really means. The honour was accepted as well-deserved, in a self-satisfying way, because it bestowed on Canadians a flattering sense of achievement. A less complacent look at the Canadian reality does not square well with this self-congratulatory stance.

There is no single measure that one can invoke to test the UN hypothesis, but there are many partial measures that would appear to indicate that the hypothesis may not be robust. Even though none of the measurements available is absolutely reliable, the sheer accumulation of bits and pieces of evidence would appear to constitute a very strong case for concern.

One may begin with an examination of the standard measure of performance in economic terms: the measurement of the real gross domestic product (GDP) per capita. A recent study by the Centre for the Study of Living Standards has shown that between 1989 and 1996, for the 13 countries of the OECD for which the Bureau of Labor Statistics produces data, Canada has recorded the worst performance in terms of real GDP per capita growth: its level was 0.4 percent lower in 1996 than in 1989. Canada ranked second to the United States in terms of GDP per capita among the 13 countries in 1989; in 1996, Canada was in seventh place. Canada's level of GDP per capita was 81.7 percent of the US level in 1986; in 1996, it had fallen to 76.7 percent (CSLS News September 1997).

There have been many important criticisms of the shortcomings of this sort of measurement. GDP does not include non-market production and leisure, is insensitive to income distribution, reflects poorly what is going on in health, education, social services and the environment, does not account for social capital, and includes many expenditures totally unrelated to economic welfare (costs related to crime or defence, for instance). This has led to more sophisticated measurements like the Nordhaus and Tobin MEW (measure of economic welfare)—that has tried to better approximate the welfare of the population by tracking more closely the population's different types of consumption. When this measure is used, the rate of growth of the real Canadian MEW per capita has proven to be much slower than the rate of growth of GDP per capita over the period 1971 to 1994. So there is no reason for celebration (Nordhaus and Tobin 1972; Messinger 1997)

An even more sophisticated and comprehensive measurement is the GPI—the Genuine Progress Indicator. It takes into account current welfare, but also the state of the natural resources, net investment, and the environment. Such an indicator shows that between 1971 and 1994, the real per capita GPI has been flat in Canada. This lack of relative progress may not be entirely surprising in light of the earlier measurements of productivity, but the complete lack of progress over such a long period can only be cause for concern (Messinger 1997).

The available measurements of social well-being are no more reassuring. A look at the ISH (Index of Social Health)—produced by Fordham's Institute for Innovation in Social Policy and focusing on the welfare of children, youth and the elderly, on the earnings but also the unemployment of adults, and on income inequalities, quality of housing, fatalities, etc.—indicates that the ISH in Canada would appear to follow more or less the same upward path as real per capita GDP up to the end of the 1970s. But, in the early 1980s, there has been a sharp discontinuity. From the 80s on, the Canadian ISH began to fall, and continued to decline until 1995—the last date for which the measurement is available—even though real GDP per capita has been growing (Miringoff 1995; Brink and Zeesman 1997). This trend reversal in the 1980s is both dramatic and puzzling. While comprehensive economic indexes would appear to remain flat or to grow relatively slowly, indicators of social well-being in Canada would appear to be deteriorating, even as the real GDP per capita increases briskly.

Things are not better when one examines the productivity data. Over the thirty-year period from the early 60s to the early 90s, Canada's annual average productivity growth has been in the neighbourhood of 1.7 percent. This ranked Canada 22nd out of the 24 OECD countries. Things did not improve in the recent past, and it would appear that, between 1989 and 1996, Canada has had the worst performance in the growth of output per person employed of the 13 OECD countries studied by the CSLS. Indeed, according to Industry Canada, since 1973, productivity growth has averaged 0.3 percent per year. At this pace, it will take 231 years for Canadians to double their standard of living.

Other indicators are not reassuring for the future either. Canada's share of foreign direct investment inward stock in the world total has declined from 8.9 percent in 1985 to 4.4 percent in 1995, as the relative attractiveness of Canada as a land of economic opportunity plummeted; and Canadian firms continue to adopt new technology much more slowly than their competitors. So one can only conclude that there are many reasons not to rest on the laurels conveyed by the UN's idyllic diagnosis.

There is no agreement on a single simple factor to explain the fact that the Canadian political socio-economy is losing ground. But one interesting hypothesis suggests that it is due to some general failure of the Canadian system to adjust its governance to the new requirements of the learning economy, and to Canada's obstinate clinging to antiquated governance structures (hierarchical and confrontational) (Valaskakis 1990; Paquet and Roy 1997).

According to this diagnosis, the Canadian socio-economy is suffering from *disconcertion*: it is disconcerted. There is a disconnection between its governance and its circumstances (Baumard 1996) that has not been noticed, and therefore has not been repaired. Indeed, as R.D. Laing would have put it, there are even reasons to believe that Canadians have failed to notice that they have failed to notice this discrepancy.

This broad diagnosis is sufficient to orient our exploration, but, in order to gauge the extent of the failures to adjust, and to delineate the sorts of repairs that the governance structure of the Canadian socio-economy needs, one must probe the features of the new economy in-the-process-of-emerging, and the characteristics of the governance it requires. This is my focus in the next section.

The Dynamics of the Learning Economy

There have been significant changes in both the environment and the texture of advanced socio-economies over the last fifty years. The environment has become much more turbulent, and information, knowledge, technology and innovation have come to play ever more important roles as central facts of life and mainsprings of progress. This has led to a flurry of efforts to measure the so-called "information sector" through its share of employment. But these efforts missed the central features in the transformation of advanced economies. The key momentous change has had much more to do with a modification of the underpinning *logic of the economy* than with a simple restructuring of its workforce.

The information or knowledge-based economy introduced a fundamental split in the economic world: a separation between the world of physical objects and the world of ideas. While many economists have denied the relevance of this split, the dynamics of these two worlds have proved so different that failure to recognize the split has derailed many well-meaning analyses. These two worlds live according to quite different rules. On the one hand, the world of physical objects is characterized by scarcity and diminishing returns, and focused mainly on allocative efficiency in a static Newtonian world. On the other hand, the world of ideas is essentially scarcity-free, inhabited by increasing returns in a quantum world, and focused on Schumpeterian efficiency (i.e., on the discontinuities in the knowledge base over time, and in the dynamic learning ability of the new evolving arrangements these entail) (Boisot 1995).

There is no completely satisfactory paradigm available yet to grapple with this post-Newtonian economy, but numerous efforts to sketch some elements of the new paradigm *en émergence*, in forums as different as the OECD and WIRED (Foray and Lundvall 1996; Kelly 1997), have made it clear that the central feature of the new post-Newtonian economy is that it is a learning economy.

A.   THE LEARNING ECONOMY

The notion of a learning economy has been developed (Lundvall and Johnson 1994) to capture the novel fact that, to a much greater extent than had been the case before, the success of individuals, firms, regions and national economies has come to depend upon their capability to learn. This is because of the accelerated rate of technical change, and the greater speed with which one has to adapt. In such a context, responsive or passive flexibility cannot suffice. What is required is *innovative flexibility*: learning, and not simply adapting (Killick 1995).

The firm, in this new setting, is defined by a bundle of competencies and capabilities. These capabilities or competencies are cumulative: they develop and improve through practice. Moreover, they embody much tacit knowledge, and depend on a social context that may be more or less supportive of effective learning. This is why it is wrong to presume that production costs do not vary across firms for the "same" productive tasks because they appear to work with the same technologies. Different firms may not have the same costs because of the fact that the tasks are not the "same" if all firms do not have the same capabilities and context.

The emergence of the learning economy has transformed the division of labour. While in the industrial world, a technical division of labour based on hyper-specialization has proved efficient, such *travail en miettes* does not promote learning. In order for learning to proceed, one must build on conversations, on work communities, and specialization must proceed to a greater extent on the basis of *craft*, i.e., of competencies. This requires a cognitive division of labour (Moati et Mouhoud 1994): a division of labour based on learning blocks (innovation systems, skill-based production fragments, etc.) that entails a very different mode of coordination.

In the old system, coordination meant standardization, and economic integration was a way to effect standardization. Subcontracting was only a form of quasi-integration. As a result, hierarchical coordination prospered. But in the new system, when the challenge is to harmonize the *capacity to learn and progress together*, the firm must focus on its core competencies, but must also consciously recognize that it operates in a business ecosystem and must mobilize its community of allies (Moore 1996).

The challenge to foster collective learning by a team calls for the development of more and more horizontal coordination of all the stakeholders. And since the relationships with the stakeholders (suppliers, customers, partners, etc.) cannot be built on simple market relations (for they may not promote efficient co-learning), *networks of relational exchanges* have emerged. In such arrangements, long-term relations based on trust are negotiated. Forms of cooperation that would never otherwise materialize evolve as a result of the emergence of important positive feedbacks and self-reinforcing mechanisms that are generated by external economies or neighbourhood effects, and learning curves that generate increasing returns (Goldberg 1989).

These dynamic processes, involving the interrelationships of many actors, generate a variety of conventions of identity and participation among these different agents. Co-learning entails co-evolution in an ecosystem that evolves by finding ways to "charter" cross-functional teams from which no important power players are left out and, if feasible, in which "all major players have some stake in the success of the strategy" (Moore 1998: 177; Arthur 1994; Krugman 1996; Durlauf 1998).

B.   COLLECTIVE LEARNING

Learning networks are a response to the need for nimbleness in the face of accelerating change, and a form of coordination capable of promoting and fostering effective learning. Organizational culture is the bond that makes these networks operative and effective at collective learning. Generally, this organizational culture embodies unwritten principles meant to generate a relatively high level of coordination at low cost by bestowing identity and membership through stories of flexible generality about events of practice that act as repositories of accumulated wisdom. The evolution of these stories constitutes collective learning, an evolving way to interpret conflicting and often confusing data, but also a social construction of a community of interpretation.

Arie de Geus uses an analogy from evolutionary biology to explain the foundations and the different phases of collective learning: the ability of individuals to move around and to be exposed to different challenges, the capacity of some individuals to invent new ways to cope creatively in the face of new circumstances, and the process of communication of the new ways from the individual to the entire community (de Geus 1997). First, a certain heterogeneity is therefore an important source of learning, since a community composed of identical individuals with similar history or experiences is less likely to extract as much new insight from a given environment. Second, research would appear to indicate that learning is not about transmission of abstract knowledge from one person's head to another person's head: it is about the "embodied ability to behave as community members", about "becoming a practitioner". Finally, learning is *legitimate peripheral participation*: it is fostered by contacts with the outside, by facilitating access to and membership in the community-of-practice of interest. (Webber 1993; Peters 1994).

Trust is at the core of both the fabric of networks and communities of practice and the new forms of shared leadership they entail. It is a way to transform "labourers into members", to convert an employment contract into a membership contract: "the concept of membership, when made real, would replace the sense of belonging to a place with a sense of belonging to a community" (Handy 1995).

Belonging is one of the most powerful agents of mobilization. So what is required is an important "moral" component to the new membership contract, that becomes less contractual and more interactive. This *new refurbished moral contract* is "a network of civic engagement...which can serve as a cultural template for future collaboration...and broaden the participants' sense of self... enhancing the participants' "taste" for collective benefits"(Putnam 1995).

Therefore, it is at the level of communities of practice that one must seek the levers to foster both learning and innovation. The challenge of the new governance for all organizations is thus not only to nurture creativity and knowledge-generating flows internally, but also to ensure that such a culture promotes connectivity externally (through networks of exchange) and the learning synergies that ensue.

C. PROXIMITIES AND LEARNING

The notions of network and community of practice entail a certain degree of interaction, and a certain degree of proximity. These are important features of the learning process.This has generated a substantial amount of interest in the multidimensional nature of proximity, for it is not clear what proximity is important for learning. More precisely, it is unclear which of the many dimensions of proximity, if any, plays the dominant role in the learning process. Some have insisted on geographical proximity, others on organizational proximity; still others have been insistent on other forms of cultural, technological or financial proximity. There is no general formula, or optimal spectrum of proximities likely to promote learning.

Depending on the sector and the moment, a mix of interaction-facilitating features of a cultural, technological, organizational or institutional nature may foster better learning. But spatial or territorial proximity fosters very strong and intensive interactions that may be necessary (even if only on a temporary basis) for organizational learning (Lazaric et Monnier 1995).

From the existing preliminary ethnographic work, we are also led to believe that the "learning region" may be much more restricted than is usually presumed on the basis of a strictly structural approach emphasizing formal jurisdictions such as provinces or states (Florida 1995; Acs, de la Mothe and Paquet 1996; Paquet 1997b). "Regional" systems of innovation may be built on communities of practice that could correspond more meaningfully to concentrated "metropolitan" areas. Yet at the same time, too strong a territorial hold on such learning networks may be counterproductive and generate lock-ins and inflexibilities that might have been avoided if the network had been more open. One may use some of Saxenian's findings on the stifling of Boston's Route 128 in the early 1990s as a cautionary tale on this front (Saxenian 1994).

Canada's Slouching toward the Learning Economy

The main points made in the last section suggest that (1) the new economy is characterized by important positive feedbacks and self-reinforcing mechanisms that generate important increasing returns to learning and co-operation; (2) the new cognitive division of labour calls for the emergence of flexible and self-organizing networks as the best loci of learning; (3) the best regime of coordination in the learning economy is less hierarchical and formal than in conventional industrial economies, and more horizontal and transversal—based on the bonds of organizational culture; and (4) in order for learning to proceed, various forms of proximity (geographic, organizational, technological, etc.) have proved important.

Yet little in the present structure and functioning of the Canadian economy, or in the policies in good currency, would appear to suggest that these conditions are present organically, or in the process of being constructed through active transformational policies. The Canadian economy remains marred by important cleavages and torn by adversary systems (federal-provincial, public-private, labour-management, small firms against one another) that have prevented it from developing into an effective learning economy (Valaskakis 1990). Indeed, the major conclusion of a recent study by the Public Policy Forum is that the most important source of Canada's low productivity growth is the lack of effective cooperation, especially between government and business (Public Policy Forum 1993). And André Burelle (1995) has shown extremely well that the federal-provincial quagmire is not far behind as a constant source of friction that prevents the development of an effective coordination/governance system.

"Since almost all learning is done by some sort of interaction, it is shaped by institutions" (Johnson 1992: 30-31): modes of interaction within firms (job rotation, on the job training, etc.) and between firms (alliances, cooperative linkages, etc.), but also relationships with other institutions (private, public and social), property rights structure, regulatory regimes, etc.

The Canadian institutions currently in place tend not to promote the development of business networks, or to improve the human infrastructure, or to enact mechanisms of industrial governance promoting collaboration. For instance, the resources dedicated to formal manpower training remain a fraction of the sums spent by our industrialized competitors in Europe and Asia: less than 20 hours per employee in Canadian companies, while it is close to 60 in Germany and around 200 in Japan. Moreover, we have not developed a capacity for cooperative linkages among the different stake-holders to the same degree that they have in the rest of the Triad; and we have an even greater hesitation to shift toward stakeholder capitalism than our American friends (de la Mothe and Paquet 1996).

Some have argued that our more diverse and heterogeneous institutional order may generate tensions, but that it is also a fount of novelty, and the source of enhanced learning. It is most certainly true that a certain degree of heterogeneity, and somewhat weaker ties, may yield more innovation than a very homogeneous order. But confrontational patterns of interaction slow down learning. Only a more flexible and consensual institutional system holds the promise of bringing "the skills, experience and knowledge of different people, organizations and government agencies together, and get[ting] them to interact in new ways" (Johnson 1992:43). But this requires an important social capital of trust and, in Canada, the social capital needed for such cooperation is eroding.

The World Values Surveys gauge very roughly the evolution of the degree of interpersonal trust and associative behaviour over the past few decades. Despite the jelly-like character of the available data, some important trends would appear to have emerged: 1) the degree of confidence and trust in one's neighbours has remained higher in Canada than in the United States; 2) there has been a significant erosion of social capital in the United States; 3) the gap between the two countries has declined, meaning a more rapid decline in Canada than in the United States; and 4) the decline of trust and associative behaviour has been even more rapid in French Canada than in the rest of Canada over this period of the post-Quiet Revolution (Paquet 1996, 1997). So, clearly there has been a significant relative erosion of the social capital of trust in Canada.

So one should not be surprised by the failure of various initiatives à la Gérald Tremblay to stimulate networks or industrial clusters in Quebec. The requisite social glue is not there, and there is little evidence that public policies have been at work to redevelop the requisite social capital for learning networks to thrive.

The same may be said about the development of "regional" innovation systems. Such systems require supporting forces from above and from below. Forces of *regionalization* (pressures of globalization and responses catalysed by a supra-local forum, such as the European Union's Committee of Regions) have encouraged these meso-level dynamics from above in other portions of the TRIAD. At the same time, the forces of *regionalism* (cultural processes of social capital and strong local identities) have facilitated action from below in the other portions of the world (Cooke, Gomez Uranga & Etxebarria 1996). In the Canadian context, these two sets of forces have not merged very well to produce a high-performance learning socio-economy.

The state has to rethink its action in the learning economy. As Dalum et al. suggest (1992), this entails intervening to improve the means to learn (education and training system), the incentive to learn (government programs supporting projects of cooperation and networks), the capability to learn (promoting organizations supporting interactive learning, i.e., more decentralized organizations), the access to relevant knowledge (through bridging the relationships between agents and sources of knowledge, both through infrastructure and mediating structures), but also fostering the requisite amount of remembering and forgetting (act to preserve competencies and capabilities, but also compensate the victims of change and make it easier for them to move ahead).

These shifts identify a new and important *didactic role* for the state. This didactic role should not be focused on predication, but on providing support for collective learning, both through the promotion of positive ways to accelerate the process, and through active engagement in dismantling obstacles to learning.

Some mistakenly view these developments as a call for the diminution of the government's role. This is not the case. States are key players with a much needed capacity to act as facilitators in governance forums, inclusive of all socio-economic actors. But they cannot be expected to do the whole job. At best, states can be important catalysts in the process of refurbishment of the coordination and governance systems. This is the central role of the *resurgent state* (Drezner 1998). But there is little evidence of any such resurgence in Canada at this time.

Canadian governments appear characterized by the existence of a centralizing mindset, and some unfortunate neglect of governance issues (Paquet 1995). Fiscal imperatives have led them to miss key opportunities (Program Review, for instance) to effect the sort of repairs to the governance system that might have gone a long way toward providing the Canadian political socio-economy with the non-centralized guidance regime it requires (Paquet and Roy 1995; Paquet and Shepherd 1996).

A Governance Challenge

On each of these fronts (negative effect of adversarial systems on social learning, slow development of the new cognitive division of labour in the workplace, a deficit of trust undermining the development of learning

networks and innovation systems, and reluctance to allow multistakeholder forums to develop), Canada's institutional framework remains
ill-adjusted to the learning economy. What is required is a number of interventions to boost the social system's adjustment process in the same
manner that a vaccine is used to boost the activity of the immune system
when it falters.

Four strategies deserve some consideration as crucial priorities: (1)
breaking down the barriers preventing the requisite partnering between
government, business and society; (2) a comprehensive knowledge-based
strategy for the new competencies-based workplace; (3) a policy for the design and support of local systems of innovation; and (4) organizational citizenship as a move toward stakeholder capitalism and better macro-social
learning.

A. OVERCOMING CANADA'S NATIONAL ADVERSARIAL SYSTEMS

Kimon Valaskakis made the point very effectively in 1990: competition is
a most effective driver that may be sufficient in a zero-sum game, but it is
not a sufficient force in a non-zero-sum game. Yet it is not easy to build the
requisite capacity to work cooperatively. Valaskakis has been tempted by a
strategy using the high road of a *mission statement* that would mobilize Canadians to act collaboratively. The failures of the Meech and
Charlottetown accords to obtain anything like the enthusiastic support of
the population might indicate, however, that this is a somewhat utopian
route.

A more promising if indirect approach is to work at eliminating many
important and deep-rooted elements that constitute the foundation of the
existing adversarial systems (Paquet 1996b). This will require a variety of
demolition tools: epistemological, legal, institutional, organizational and
existential.While this is not the place to develop a comprehensive review of
those tools, at least a few words about some possible initiatives are in order.

One of the first targets should be an attack on a most important assumption buried in the current North American ethos, and well expounded
by Jane Jacobs in her book *Systems of Survival* (1992). The ethos in good
currency in North America lionizes competition. Collaboration is either
ruled impossible or declared a great source of concern: according to Jacobs, the commercial moral syndrome and the guardian moral syndrome
are so diametrically opposed that any mix can only produce "monstrous
hybrids".

To rehabilitate cooperation at the epistemological level, it is therefore
essential first to show that it may work conceptually as an appropriate

learning strategy. This is the argument that Brandenburger and Nalebuff's *Co-opetition* (1996) has put forward, using a non-zero-sum game theoretical framework. Their argument covers the case of all the partners and "complementers" in the value net. But there will not be a mindquake unless one can demonstrate that cooperation is not only conceptually possible, but that it works effectively and with much benefit in a variety of empirical contexts. Fortunately, this has already been argued most eloquently by Axelrod (1984) and Ostrom (1990), so one can make the case for cooperation persuasively. But it must be clearly explained.

Secondly, one must also modify the legal framework so that it is not prohibiting or discouraging cooperation. For instance, the tradition of *absolute* property rights of shareholders in the English-speaking world, the nature of the existing corporation law, and the present antitrust regulatory framework are not conducive to such arrangements of cooperation (de la Mothe and Paquet 1996).

Finally, the insistence on the *formality* of explicit market contracts enforceable by courts, in the Canadian tradition, has had important consequences for the sort of organizational and existential arrangements that have been allowed to prevail. In Canada, we are still a long way from being able to operate in a world of *contractual governance* where relationships based on implicit, relational contracting (that are informally enforced) are accorded as much credibility and legitimacy as more explicit contracts (Blair 1995; Kester 1992). Transforming our legal philosophy will be quite a task. Modifications to the legal and institutional orders that would make possible new federal/provincial forums à la Burelle, or new forms of government-business-society relations, or greater labour-management cooperation, etc. will undoubtedly make cooperation less difficult. But the emergence of a true cooperative spirit may have to wait until we have also transformed many more organizational features of our business system, as, for instance, (1) the structure of our accounting practices and financial reporting to measure more precisely the different forms of intangible assets embodied in alliances and partnerships and (2) the present financial statements to ensure that they reveal more clearly how the surplus has been shared among the stakeholders (Perrin 1975 ; Gerlach 1992; Sveiby 1997).

Even a large number of such changes in the rules of the game will not automatically transform the ethos of the Canadian political socio-economy, but they will help in reframing the *dominant logic* (Prahalad and Bettis 1986; Bettis and Prahalad 1995)—the way the environment is described and represented, and the way that debates and argumentations are conducted in the socio-economy. This cannot be effected, as the utopians suggest, by sheer tinkering with institutions and organizations. What is required is a truly fundamental change in the basic social norms of the community, in the corporate culture, in the very notion of the "game" Canadian citizens are involved in. But, very often, a transformation in the *technology* of the social system triggers a modification in the *structure* of the system, and even in the *theory* of the system, i.e., in the definition of what the system is in the business of doing, in its dominant logic (Schon 1971).

In fact, the *dominant logic* will have to be transformed in stages, through a process of piecemeal modifications that deal with subsectors separately. This is the rationale for the proactive interventions suggested below in the worlds of work, local systems of innovation, and citizenship. And much time is bound to be required before one can hope to bring forth the new social contract of cooperation, and the new institutional order that is sought in the long run—the one capable of jointly maximizing, through cooperation, wealth creation, social cohesion and political freedom in a learning socio-economy (Dahrendorf 1995).

In the meantime, more modest goals must be accepted in the short run. One may have to be satisfied with reaching only for some minimal tact and civility, a decent society—"one whose institutions do not humiliate people"—on the way to a civilized society—"one whose members do not humiliate one another" (Kingwell 1995; Margalit 1996), and for reforms bringing forth some mix of institutions that would at least ensure that much.

These modest short-run goals are so remote from the ultimate objective of a social contract of cooperation that some may be discouraged. But one must recognize one of the consequences of the balkanization of the social terrain into many disconnected fragments (Piore 1995) may well be that the sort of consensus on common goals, across society, that might be regarded as the first-best solution for a learning society (Keating 1995:224), will prove unachievable. One may have to settle on second-best solutions, entailing the coexistence of many dominant logics in different portions of the social terrain, and some form of viable *arrimage* among them that might contribute to the creation of a reasonably stable reference point—some unity through diversity.

B. WORK AS SELF-ACTIVITY

Cognition and learning are processes through which individuals and organizations are transformed, and in some way produce themselves as they evolve. Work is self-activity, self-creation.

One of the most important challenges to the Canadian governance system is the development of a series of supporting institutions for the world of cognition and work in the learning economy. As mentioned earlier, the learning economy is transforming the division of labour. The new cognitive division of labour (based on cognitive blocks) has generated a new world of work. In the world of ideas, cognition and the production of new knowledge—the process of extraction of information from the environment through perception, and the development of knowledge through communication—are of central importance. In the cases of both the individual and the organization, cognition takes the form of a pattern (neural network or social network) and learning is a transformation of these patterns (cognitive representations) in the form of neural nets, routines or conventions (Paquet 1998).

The need for flexibility as a result of accelerated change has translated into a two-stage process of change in the workplace. First, the need for nimbleness has led to a workplace characterized by contingent workers that are more and more often in business for themselves, and must engage in self-development and lifelong learning as a way to retain their employability. It is a world where the permanent 9 to 5 job ensured for a lifetime is becoming less and less the norm. A larger and larger portion of the population is involved in non-conventional work, as the learning economy challenges the old way of organizing work (Bridges 1994). Second, since innovation and learning are central in the new economy, there has been a reintegration of these fragments of the production process into more meaningful "knowledge blocks", characterized both by creative synergies and much creativity, but dynamically compatible with other "knowledge blocks" and capable of progressing in concert with them in localized systems of innovation, as we will see in the next section (Moati and Mouhoud 1994:59).

Indeed, one may consider this section and the next one as corresponding roughly to two phases in the process of transformation in the division of labour: the fragmentation phase and the synergy phase.

In the short run, in the fragmentation phase, a number of initiatives can easily facilitate the transition to the new world.

For the worker, it becomes extremely important to be able to count on a revision of tax laws that would recognize individuals more and more as businesses. This would not only promote a greater awareness of income as return on human capital, and self-development as an investment, but make the worker more conscious that employability is now the worker's responsibility.For firms, the incentive not to cooperate with workers in developing their human capital (for fear that enhanced employees would simply be stolen by other firms) has to be countered by programs limiting free riding through tax credits that will ensure that those who do not train their employees are hit by higher taxes. For government, the new role of providing transitional help (to retrain, relocate, start a business), over and beyond in-stituting a framework to support workers and employers in their learning initiatives, should also lead to detaching the safety net from the "job", and to an end to pouring energy into the fantasy of creating permanent jobs.

In the longer run, in the fragmentation phase, what is required is a dra-matic reframing of our perspectives on work as self-activity. Instead of clinging to antiquated versions of the labour market as locus of exchange of more or less homogeneous lumps of human capital, one has to recognize that, if knowledge and competence are so central to the new cognitive divi-sion of labour, one must

(a)   develop the machinery necessary to gain a much better image of the existing stock of knowledge and competence available, and not only of the lumps of human labour for hire;

(b)   ensure that the gaps between the supply and demand of skills, competences, capabilities, etc., can be more effectively corrected by the development of *new* abilities, competencies and capabilities, or of entirely *new blocks of knowledge* to meet the demands of firms, industries or regions;

(c)   but also, and more importantly perhaps, adopt a much broader *problématique* in which work is defined as self-activity, based on a lifelong learning process deeply rooted in early childhood, and in the material conditions in which the individual has developed his/her capabilities to acquire savoir, savoir-faire and savoir-être.

This calls for a dramatic broadening of the notion of learning and com-petences, and suggests that two important initiatives should be undertaken in parallel: (1) the development of a new information system to ensure greater efficiency in the allocation of competences, and a better guidance system in the new production of knowledge; (2) a broader perspective on the world of work as self-activity, or personal development, with, as a mat-ter of consequence, greater attention being given to the care of children as a first step in developing a strong cognitive economy, i.e., an economy that makes the highest and best use of all the brainpower coming its way.

(1) The sort of new information system geared to generating a better knowledge system has already been sketched in a most innovative way by Authier and Lévy (1992). In their book, the authors call for more comprehensive inventories of the existing stock of knowledge of all types

(technical or not, formal or tacit, knowledge, savoir-faire or savoir-être, etc.) held by individuals and communities. They show how images of these complex profiles could easily be stored in the magnetic band of an individual citizen card (in lieu of the information-poor traditional curriculum vitae) and aggregated into a knowledge tree that would summarize the competences of a community (basic knowledge in the trunk, more specialized knowledge in the branches, and very specialized knowledge in the leaves). This approach would allow not only a composite cognitive portrait of each community, but an aggregation of these cognitive maps regionally or nationally.

These composite portraits of the available competencies could easily be compared with the data bank of ideal profiles of competences as defined by employers on the basis of their most recent production arrangements. This would reveal the communities' competences and knowledge gaps, and serve as an important compass in determining the different gradients that should guide the new production of knowledge and competences, and the exploration of new terrains. What would ensue is nothing less than a *knowledge/competences exchange,* that would correspond much more closely to what is needed in the learning economy than the clumsy interventions to fit square bundles of competencies into round employment opportunities.

For the time being, there is no global strategy to cope with the new realities of the workplace. Moreover, there is little awareness that such an approach, based on competencies and capabilities, requires a new unit of analysis (savoirs, savoir-faire, savoir-être) instead of the old category of worker, and that it will have to be developed jointly by workers, employers, communities and governments, for without their full cooperation (on matters involving privacy and the like) the scheme is clearly unworkable.

One may imagine a complete reframing of the way in which our society would deal with dropouts, unemployment, and exclusion if this sort of approach were to be used. The only initiative that would appear to come close to adopting such a perspective (only partially and only in certain more enlightened versions of the scheme) has been workfare: a social innovation built on a recognition that dealing effectively with exclusion requires a complete reframing of the workplace *problématique* and a mobilization of the community (Paquet and Roy 1998).

(2)   But the highest and best use of available competences alone remains too narrow and static a perspective. Learning is more encompassing than the mere reshuffling of the competence deck. It must address the central problem of the production of knowledge, and this pertains to the mutual interaction between the individual and the environment throughout

his/her lifetime.This underlines the importance of the social environment in the production of new knowledge, but also the need to take into account the importance of healthy communities as foundations of a learning society.

This in turn will impact the developmental process of children and the requirement for adequate nurturing as a fundamental element in a learning society. Effective learning societies need to support lifelong learning throughout the population (from early childhood on, and most importantly, at the time of early childhood) if they wish to make the highest and best use of all the brainpower coming their way.

Keating (1995) has conducted an extensive program of research in which this broader perspective has been brought to bear on the challenges of the information society, and he has shown that Japan and much of Europe appear to foster more supportive environments in early childhood and adolescence, but also provide support for lifelong learning that are much better than what is available in the UK, the USA, and Canada.

Tackling the problem at this level means developing a *problématique* of personal development that has little to do with the usual labour market fables. This would require an integration of much of the work currently done in medicine, education, psychology and sociology along with the traditional concerns of labour market economics, to underpin a global strategy of intervention on this broad human-capital-and-learning front. It would permit an escape from the present black hole emanating from the separate discussions by experts in these different disciplines.

What is at stake here is the development of a new approach that would take a comprehensive view of work as self-activity, and would tackle the problem of learning as a lifelong social phenomenon that requires new conventions and rules pertaining to the whole life cycle of individuals, and to the whole range of networks and organizations in which individuals learn. This sort of broad and comprehensive approach cannot be simply the result of a government policy. It must be arrived at jointly by the different stakeholders (families, health officials, firms, social capital specialists, labour organizations, educational specialists, etc.) in a diversity of forums where, in a complementary but integrated way, the issues of lifelong learning and of the new production of knowledge may be debated, and dynamically compatible approaches can be developed (de la Mothe and Paquet 1997).

C. LOCAL SYSTEMS OF INNOVATION

In an economy dynamized by information, knowledge, competence and capabilities, the new relevant units of analysis of the production process have to be those that serve as the basis for understanding and nurturing innovation. Focusing either on the firm or on the national economy would appear to be equally misguided: under the microscope, too much is idiosyncratic and white noise is bound to run high; under the macroscope, much of the innovation and restructuring going on is bound to be missed. One must therefore argue that the most useful perspective point is the Schumpeterian/Dahmenian *meso-perspective* focusing on development blocks, sub-national forums, etc., where the learning is really occurring (de la Mothe and Paquet 1994).

In an evolutionary model, the process of learning and discovery is only one blade of the pair of scissors. The other blade is the interactive mechanism with the context or environment through which selection occurs. This interactive mechanism is fitness-driven: firm search processes "both provide the source of differential fitness—firms whose R&D turn up more profitable processes of production or products will grow relative to their competitors—and tend to bind them together as a community" (Dosi and Nelson 1994:162).

Both on the organization side, and on the forum/environment side, proximity breeds interaction and socio-economic learning (Boswell 1990). Moreover, these interactive mechanisms are fuelled by dynamic increasing returns to agglomeration. In most cases, these agglomeration economies are bounded, and therefore do not give rise to monopoly by a single region or location, but they generate snowballing increasing returns (Arthur 1990). And the state has much to do as a catalyst on both fronts, but especially with the nature of context.

We do not know as much as we should about the innovation process, the process of learning and discovery, and the process of diffusion of technical and organizational innovations. But as Nelson and Winter (1977) suggested, at the core of these processes is the notion of "selection environment" which is defined as the context that "determines how relative use of different technologies changes over time" (p.61). This context is shaped by market and non-market components, conventions, socio-cultural factors, and by the broader institutional structure. This selection environment constitutes the relevant milieu in explaining the innovative capacity of a sector/region.

The notion of milieu has been defined as "un ensemble territorial formé de réseaux intégrés de ressources matérielles et immatérielles, dominé par une culture historiquement constituée, vecteur de savoirs et savoir-faire, et reposant sur un système relationnel de type coopération/concurrence des acteurs localisés" (Lecoq 1989). Consequently, the notion of milieu suggests three sets of forces: (1) the contours of a particular spatial set vested with a certain unity and tonus; (2) the organizational logic of a network of interdependent actors engaged in cooperative innovative activity; and (3) organizational learning based on the dialectics between the <u>internal milieu</u> and the <u>external milieu</u> (Maillat 1992).

There are innovations and considerable learning even in the absence of a <u>dynamic milieu</u>, but such a <u>milieu</u> is likely to bring forth innovation networks; and innovation networks, in turn, are a hybrid form of organization so much better adapted to conditions of technological and appropriation uncertainty than markets or hierarchies, that they are more likely to kick-start the innovation process.

At the core of the <u>dynamic milieu,</u> and of the innovation network, are a number of intermingled dimensions (economic, historical, cognitive and normative) but they all depend to a certain degree on *trust and confidence*, and therefore on a host of cultural and sociological factors that have a tendency to be found mainly in localized networks, and to be more likely to emerge in a background of shared experiences, regional loyalties, etc. This is *social capital*, and it plays a central role in meso-systems' dynamics and in their capacity to learn and transform.

There must be a series of initiatives spearheaded by the government, but in close collaboration with the other stakeholders, to promote a non-centralized governance process likely to build important pillars on which local systems of innovation can thrive. These initiatives should be mainly steered by collectives of firms (like the Ottawa Centre for Research and Innovation, for instance) at the local level, but supported by *regionalization drives* from higher order governments. And since <u>dynamic milieux</u> are likely to be local or regional systems of innovation, they should be targeted not only for support, but for proactive interventions to generate the requisite multistakeholder forums needed to underpin their development and progress (de la Mothe and Paquet 1998).

Much must also be done to foster *strategic regionalism and localism* (Roy 1998) by nurturing already existing local dynamics. As Storper argues, "in technologically dynamic production complexes ... there is a strong reason for the existence of regional clusters or agglomerations. Agglomeration appears to be a principal geographical form in which the trade-off between lock-in technological flexibility (and the search for quasi-rents), and cost minimization can be most effectively managed, because it facilitates efficient operations of a cooperative production network" (Storper 1992:84). But Storper adds that "codes, channels of interaction, and ways of organizing and coordinating behaviors"—all matters pertaining to governance—are what make learning possible (p.85). The confluence of issues (learning, networks, lock-in, conventions and types of knowledge) must be rooted in political-economic cultures, rules and institutions, and in most countries these are highly differentiated at the regional level. Such forces must be harnessed.

Canada, the USA, and Mexico are countries where one may reasonably detect a mosaic of political-economic cultures, rules and conventions with differential innovative potential (Maddox and Gee 1994). Consequently, one may say that there is a genuine "territorialization of learning", and that spatial proximity is likely to play a fundamental role in the system of innovation (de la Mothe and Paquet 1998). This, in turn, suggests that the appropriate governance system likely to generate a higher degree of innovativeness is non-centralized, and more local and regional than national.

D.   ORGANIZATIONAL CITIZENSHIP

There is considerable merit in dismantling the impediments to cooperation, in facilitating as much as possible the emergence of cognitive maps and knowledge/competence exchanges, in rethinking the notion of work as self-activity in the context of personal development, and in fostering robust local systems of innovation. But it is unlikely that these initiatives will reverberate throughout the socio-economy unless one tackles the important problem of organizational citizenship.

At the core of the new governance stands a refurbished notion of active citizenship that encompasses not only individuals but organizations, for it would be naive to believe that, in a learning economy and society so crucially based on collective (community, network, etc.) learning, the traditional notion of individual citizenship à la T.H. Marshall (1965) can suffice. Too many collectives play a crucial role: communities of practice and local systems (binding them into communities of interpretation) (Paquet 1989). A focus on individual rights leaves too much of what is going on in the learning economy out of the equation.

In the new economy, the individual takes part in a variety of teams and clubs, and this leads to a fragmentation of the self into a large number of limited identities. It is only through the imbrication and re-articulation of these limited identities that one may hope to reconstruct some common ethos. Unfortunately, this cannot be accomplished through anything like the traditional social consensus on common goals across society—the new overarching social consensus that many are still dreaming about (Keating 1995:225).

It must rather be a new form of strong sociality, built on weak links, on a multiplicity of distributed, non-centralized, collaborative and adaptive meso-organizations over which the citizen is more or less spread, and constituting of necessity an always incomplete and evolving interactional collectivity (Paquet 1994). This second-best approach to creative collaboration is built on a modicum of unanimity around certain separate foci, and on the recognition that these are the new units of analysis—the new (local, sectorial, regional, sectional, transversal, national, etc.) networks which have succeeded in generating partial and yet substantive loyalties, on which the more encompassing sense of belonging is built.

But how can there be any construction of a new composite citizenship on these partial organizations unless the organizations themselves are recognized as having rights and obligations? There is, at this time, a certain capacity to demand accountability from government by the global financial markets, by the multinationals, and by a variety of important nonstate organizations defending certain human rights (Sassen 1996). Surely a good case could be made for providing these organizations (but also many other less threatening organizations) with a new form of citizenship that would formally recognize the existence of their *de facto* rights, and establish commensurate de facto obligations and responsibilities that they would have to meet in order for these rights to be legitimized.

This new form of *organizational citizenship* is meant to serve as a basis for the construction of a meaningful new ethos *par morceau*. For it is only through these meso-social armistices (embodied in networks that are not necessarily territoriallly bound) that succeed in establishing some "regional" equilibria in portions of the terrain, that one may hope to construct a more global notion of citizenship. What will ensue is "une *persona* que l'on forge au fur et à mesure que l'on vit et pense au milieu de ses concitoyens ... *un système de différences partagées* que ses membres reconnaissent" (Drummond 1981-2).

In this context, the individual has rights and obligations, but citizenship is not exhausted by this smallest unit: it fits within a succession of ever larger organizational units that also have rights and responsibilities at each level.

First, this notion of organizational citizenship has the merit of operationalizing the optionalist version of citizenship: the notion that citizenship is acquired by consent and cumulatively through the addition of layer after layer of commitments through the organizations one joins in some way. Citizenship becomes the outcome of accumulated memberships and provides, by aggregation, a very distributed and variegated notion of citizenship that is very well adjusted to a society of multiple identities.

Second, another important merit of the concept of *organizational citizenship* is that it would press organizations to take into account the full range of their stakeholders in negotiating their ensemble of rights and responsibilities, because otherwise they would risk their organizational citizenship's being denied. In that way, organizations will come to represent genuine partial social armistices among stakeholders that would help construct piecemeal a more comprehensive representation for the multiple selves of individual citizens.

Third, this approach would have the merit of allowing a nexus of moral contracts to be negotiated among concerns that are non-trivial, i.e., the concerns that possess organizational capital enabling them to exert pressure on and demand accountability from the state. The ensuing web of moral contracts would constitute the texture of the national or multinational citizenship in various terrains. The European Union might be a good example.

This new, piecemeal, bottom-up citizenship, if it works well, generates "webs of voluntary, mutual responsibility" (Tracy Kidder, quoted by Bennis and Biederman 1997:19) and creates the requisite new social ligatures capable of generating both a new division of labour, and a new capacity to collaborate. Organizational citizenship is a form of loose and fluid contractualization, a permanent process of negotiation and social learning. It allows the sort of adjustment in the social ligatures that is best adapted to circumstances, while ensuring the modicum of coherence and persistence of the institutional order necessary to integrate realities that would otherwise appear unlikely to cohere. This sort of collective coordination, based on appeals to solidaristic values and collective goods, institutionalizes various arrangements that provide an environment that supports cooperation at the lower level (Hollingsworth 1993).

This sort of arrangement may leave many readers uneasy because of its corporatist flavour. There is undoubtedly some such element in the notion of organizational citizenship, as there is in any social governance arrangement built on negotiation and consensus. Yet if there is a community of interests, communities have rights and can have obligations. These community rights obviously limit individual rights. But while they appear to exist de facto, it does not seem that adding responsibilities to de facto rights does anything but somewhat temper those collective rights. Pluralists should therefore not be outraged.

In the absence of an overall switching mechanism, capable of shifting the system between regimes depending on places, times and circumstances, our social system has to learn how to live with multiple and partially contradictory logics. Canada's governance system must learn to live with multiple, partially contradictory cognitive maps: from these local partial logics, a new sense of solidarity can emerge bottom-up, if indeed it can emerge at all (Paquet 1995b). This is the basis of this gamble on *organizational citizenship*.

Conclusion

Canadian standards of living have become tied to our ability to learn. And since our performance has not improved much recently, and may have deteriorated somewhat according to certain indicators, there are reasons to fear that our socio-economic system may be suffering from learning disabilities. There are many hypotheses to explain Canada's lacklustre performance (a techno-economic revolution requiring a much greater investment to generate the same increase in output; global competition; failure of government; failure of leadership in the private sector; a decline in social capital à la Putnam; etc.). These are all indicators of a failure to adapt well to new circumstances, of a failure in our capacity to transform, and ultimately of a failure of the coordination/governance system to fit the new requirements of the learning economy.

This is not unique to Canada and many leading institutions in other countries have already reacted by creating special programs of research to study the failures of the national governance system. In 1996, the John F. Kennedy School of Government at Harvard began an ambitious multi-year project to clarify thinking about governance in the 21st century. Perhaps, this is a challenge that the Royal Society of Canada should rise to.

Everywhere the central question is the same: in what way can one rebuild the governance regime to improve the performance of the socio-economy?

I have examined the dynamics of the new learning economy, and tried to identify in what ways Canada might have failed in developing the appropriate sort of organizational and institutional infrastructure that would be necessary for learning to proceed effectively. I have also identified four areas where urgent action might be required.

These policy fields are wide ranging, and the interventions required all depend on a reframing of our perspective on governance.

The levers identified cannot be used without changing the nature of the game:

(1) nurturing government-business-society collaboration as a major source of productivity increase means an abandonment of the ethos of competition;

(2) rethinking the workplace as an information/competences exchange, but also as the locus for work as self-activity and lifelong learning, involves the abandonment of the old labour market frameworks;

(3) betting on local systems of innovation as the locus of creative adaptation and innovation requires a rethinking of the centrality of the old nation state; and

(4) organizational citizenship paves the way for a building of a new sociality *par morceau,* and rejects the icon of absolute individualism.

This is why changing the governance regime will require first of all a revolution in the mind of Canadian leaders before we can hope for action on these fronts, and a capacity to recognize that the usual tinkering tactics will no longer suffice.

Such a radical mindquake is not to be expected as a matter of course. It usually emerges as a result of major catastrophes or scandals. Consequently, we need the moral equivalent of a war, or the sociological equivalent of a catastrophe, or a surge of creative leadership.

In the meantime, the very idea of these reforms remains a taboo topic. Since Canada is the country with the best quality of life in the world, why would anyone in his/her right mind wish to embark on a series of radical and probably politically unpopular reforms to fix something that ain't broken!

References

Z.Acs, J. de la Mothe and G. Paquet (1996) "Local Systems of Innovation: Toward an Enabling Strategy" in P. Howitt (Ed.) *The Implications of Knowledge-based Growth for Microeconomic Policies*, Calgary:University of Calgary Press, pp. 339-358 .

W.B. Arthur (1990) "'Silicon Valley' Locational Clusters: When Do Increasing Returns Imply Monopoly?" *Mathematical Social Sciences*, 19, pp. 235-251.

W.B. Arthur (1994) *Increasing Returns and Path Dependence in the Economy*. Ann Arbor: The University of Michigan Press.

M. Authier and P. Lévy (1992) *Les arbres de connaissances*. Paris: La Découverte.

R. Axelrod (1984) *The Evolution of Cooperation*. New York: Basic Books.

P. Baumard (1996) *Organizations déconcertées*. Paris: Masson.

W. Bennis and P.W. Biederman (1997) *Organizing Genius: The Secrets of Creative Collaboration*. Reading, Mass: Addison-Wesley.

R.A. Bettis et C.K. Prahalad (1995) "The Dominant Logic: Retrospective and Extension" *Strategic Management Journal*, 16, pp. 5-14.

M.M. Blair (1995) *Ownership and Control—Rethinking Corporate Governance for the Twentieth Century*. Washington: The Brookings Institution.

M. Boisot (1995) *Information Space: A Framework for Learning in Organizations, Institutions and Culture*. London:Routledge.

J. Boswell (1990) *Community and the Economy*. London: Routledge.

A.M. Brandenburger and B.J. Nalebuff (1996) *Co-opetition*. New York: Currency Doubleday.

W. Bridges (1994) *JobShift*. Reading, Mass.: Addison-Wesley

S. Brink and A. Zeesman (1997) *Measuring Social Well-Being: An Index of Social Health for Canada*. HRDC Working Papers. June 57p.

A. Burelle (1995) *Le mal canadien*. Montréal: Fides.

CSLS News (1997) Newsletter of the Centre for the Study of Living Standards, September.

P.Cooke, M.G. Uranga, and G. Etxebarria (1996) "The Regional and Institutional Dimension of Innovation Systems" EAEPE 1996 Conference, Antwerp, November 1996 (mimeo 17p.)

R. Dahrendorf (1995) "A Precarious Balance: Economic Opportunity, Civil Society, and Political Liberty" *The Responsive Community*, 5, 3, pp. 13-39.

B. Dalum et al. (1992) "Public Policy in the Learning Society" in B. Lundvall (Ed.) *National Systems of Innovation*. London: Pinter, pp. 296-317.

A. de Geus (1997) "The Living Company" *Harvard Business Review*, 75, 2, pp. 51-59.

J. de la Mothe and G. Paquet (1994) "The Technology-Trade Nexus: Liberalization, Warring Blocs, or Negotiated Access?" *Technology in Society*, 16, 1, pp. 97-118.

J. de la Mothe and G. Paquet (eds) (1996) *Corporate Governance and the New Competition*. Ottawa: PRIME.

J. de la Mothe and G.Paquet (eds) (1997) *Challenges Unmet in the New Production of Knowledge*.Ottawa: PRIME.

J. de la Mothe and G.Paquet (eds) (1998) *Local and Regional Systems of Innovation*. Boston: Kluwer Academic Publishers (in press)

G. Dosi and R.R. Nelson (1994) "An Introduction to Evolutionary Theories in Economics" *Journal of Evolutionary Economics*, 4, 3, pp. 153-172.

D. Drezner (1998) "The Resurgent State" *The Washington Quarterly*, 21, 1, pp. 209-225.

L. Drummond (1981-2) "Analyse sémiotique de l'ethnicité au Québec" *Question de culture*, No. 2, pp. 139-153

S.N. Durlauf (1998) "What Should Policymakers Know about Economic Complexity?" *The Washington Quarterly*, 21, 1, pp. 157-165.

R. Florida (1995) "Toward the Learning Region" *Futures*, 27, 5, pp. 527-536.

D. Foray and B.A. Lundvall (1996) "The Knowledge-Based Economy: From the Economics of Knowledge to the Learning Economy" in *Employment and Growth in the Knowledge-Based Economy*. Paris: OECD, pp. 11-32.

M.L. Gerlach (1992) *Alliance Capitalism*. Berkeley: University of California Press.

V.P. Goldberg (1989) *Readings in the Economics of Contract Law*. Cambridge: Cambridge University Press.

C. Handy (1995) "Trust and the Virtual Organization" *Harvard Business Review*, 73, 3, pp. 40-50.

J.H. Holland (1995) *Hidden Order*. Reading, Mass.: Addison-Wesley.

R. Hollingsworth (1993) "Variations Among Nations in the Logic of Manufacturing Sectors and International Competitiveness" in D. Foray and C. Freeman (eds) *Technology and the Wealth of Nations*. London: Pinter, pp. 301-321.

J.Jacobs (1992) *Systems of Survival*. New York: Random House.

B. Johnson (1992) "Institutional Learning" in B. Lundvall (Ed.) *National Systems of Innovation*. London: Pinter, pp. 23-44.

D.P. Keating (1995) "The Learning Society in the Information Age" in S.A. Rosell et al. *Changing Maps: Governing in a World of Rapid Change*. Ottawa: Carleton University Press, pp. 205-229.

K. Kelly (1997) "New Rules for the New Economy" WIRED, 5, 09, 140-197.

W.C. Kester (1992) "Industrial Groups as Systems of Contractual Governance" *Oxford Review of Economic Policy*, 8, 3, pp. 24-44.

T. Killick (1995) *The Flexible Economy*. London : Routledge.

M. Kingwell (1995) *A Civil Tongue*. University Park, Penn.:The Pennsylvania State University Press.

P. Krugman (1996) *The Self-Organizing Economy*. Oxford: Blackwell

N. Lazaric et J.M. Monnier (eds) (1995) *Coordination économique et apprentissage des firmes*. Paris: Economica

B. Lecoq (1989) *Réseau et système productif régional*. Dossiers de l'IRER, 23.

B. Lundvall and B. Johnson. (1994) "The Learning Economy" *Journal of Industry Studies*, 1, pp. 23-42

J.Maddox and H. Gee (1994) "Mexico's Bid to Join the World" *NATURE*, 28 April, pp. 789-804.

D. Maillat (1992) "Milieux et dynamique territoriale de l'innovation. *Canadian Journal of Regional Science*, XV, 2, pp. 199-218.

A. Margalit (1996) *The Decent Society*. Cambridge: Harvard University Press.

T.H. Marshall (1965) *Class, Citizenship and Social Development*. New York: Anchors Books

H. Messinger (1997) *Measuring Sustainable Economic Welfare: Looking Beyond GDP*. Paper presented at the annual meeting of the CEA (St. John's Newfoundland) June, 22p.

M.L. Miringoff (1995) *Index of Social Health*. Tarrytown, N.Y: Fordham Institute for Innovation in Social Policy.

P. Moati et E.M. Mouhoud (1994) "Information et organization de la production: vers une division cognitive du travail" *Économie appliquée*, 46, 1, pp. 47-73.

J.F. Moore (1996) *The Death of Competition*. New York: Harper Collins.

J.F. Moore (1998) "The Rise of a New Corporate Form" *The Washington Quarterly*, 21, 1, pp. 167-181.

R.R. Nelson and S.G. Winter (1977) "In Search of a Useful Theory of Innovation" *Research Policy*, 6, 1, pp. 36-76.

W.D.Nordhaus and J. Tobin (1972) "Is Growth Obsolete?" In *Economic Research: Retrospect and Prospect*. Fiftieth Anniversary Colloquium, Vol. V. New York: National Bureau of Economic Research, pp. 1-80.

E. Ostrom (1990) *Governing the Commons*. Cambridge: Cambridge University Press.

G. Paquet (1989) "Pour une notion renouvelée de citoyenneté" *Mémoires de la Société royale du Canada, Série V*, Tome IV , pp. 83-100.

G. Paquet (1994) "La citoyenneté dans la société d'information: une réalité transversale et paradoxale" *Mémoires de la Société royale du Canada*, Série VI, Tome V, pp. 59-78.

G.Paquet (1995) "Gouvernance distribuée et habitus centralisateur" *Mémoires de la Société royale du Canada*, Série VI, Tome VI, pp. 93-107.

G. Paquet (1995b) "Institutional Evolution in an Information Age" in T.J. Courchene (ed.) *Technology, Information and Public Policy—The Bell Canada Papers on Economic and Public Policy*, 3. Kingston: John Deutsch Institute for the Study of Economic Policy, pp. 197-229.

G. Paquet (1996) "La grisaille institutionnelle" in S. Coulombe et G.Paquet (eds) *La ré-invention des institutions et le rôle de l'état*. Montréal:Association des économistes québécois, pp.393-421

G. Paquet (1996b) "The Downtrodden Administrative Route" *Inroads,* # 5, pp.117-121.
G. Paquet (1997) "Et si la Révolution Tranquille n'avait pas eu lieu..." *L'Agora*, 4, 2, pp. 35-36.
G. Paquet (1997b) "States, Communities and Markets: The Distributed Governance Scenario" in T.J. Courchene (ed) *The Nation State in a Global/Information Era: Policy Challenges—The Bell Canada Papers on Economic and Public Policy*, 5. Kingston: John Deutsch Institute for the Study of Economic Policy, pp. 25-46.
G. Paquet (1998) "Evolutionary Cognitive Economics" in *Information Economics and Policy* (in press)
G.Paquet and J. Roy (1995) "Prosperity Through Networks: The Small Business Strategy That Might Have Been" in S. Phillips (Ed.) *How Ottawa Spends—Midlife Crises*. Ottawa: Carleton University Press, pp. 137-158.
G. Paquet and J. Roy (1997) *Governance in Canada. (Version V)* Ottawa: PRIME
G. Paquet and J. Roy (1998) "Workfare as Social Innovation" (Working paper of the Centre on Governance)
G. Paquet and R. Shepherd (1996) "The Program Review Process: A Deconstruction" in G. Swimmer (Ed.) *How Ottawa Spends - Life Under the Knife*. Ottawa: Carleton University Press, pp. 39-72.
J.Perrin (1975) "Pour un nouveau tableau de bord de l'entreprise" *Revue française de gestion*, no. 2, pp. 35-40.
T. Peters (1994) *Crazy Times Call For Crazy Organizations*.New York: Vintage Books
M.J. Piore (1995) *Beyond Individualism*. Cambridge: Harvard University Press.
C.K. Prahalad et R.A. Bettis (1986) "The Dominant Logic: A New Linkage Between Diversity and Performance" *Strategic Management Journal*, 7, pp. 485-501.
Public Policy Forum (1993) *Private-Public Sector Cooperation as a Means of Improving a Country's Economic Performance*: *A Survey of Practices in Canada, the US, Europe and Japan*. Ottawa: Public Policy Forum.
R.D. Putnam (1995) "Bowling Alone: America's Declining Social Capital" *Journal of Democracy*, 6, 1, pp.65-78.
J. Roy (1998) "Canada's Technology Triangle: Traditional Government and Synergistic Governance" in J. de la Mothe and G.Paquet (eds) *Local and Regional Systems of Innovation*. Boston: Kluwer Academic Publishers (in press)
S. Sassen (1996) *Losing Control? Sovereignty in an Age of Globalization*. New York: Columbia University Press.
A. Saxenian (1994) *Regional Advantage*. Cambridge: Harvard University Press.
D.A. Schon (1971) *Beyond the Stable State*. New York: Norton.
M. Storper (1992) "The Limits of Globalization: Technology Districts and International Trade" *Economic Geography*, 68, 1, pp. 60-93.
K. E. Sveiby (1997) *The New Organizational Wealth*. San Francisco: Berrett-Koehler.
K. Valaskakis (1990) *Canada in the Nineties*. Montreal: The Gamma Institute Press.
A.M. Webber (1993) "What's So New About the New Economy" *Harvard Business Review*, 71, 1, pp. 24-42.

THOMAS J. COURCHENE, FRSC

Canadian Federalism in Transition: An Ontario Perspective

Abstract

Ontario is evolving from its traditional role as Canada's "heartland" to become a North American region state, i.e., an economic powerhouse characterized by cross-border activity and increasingly orienting its policies and focus towards North America. This concept is already well understood in Europe, where the Lyon / Turin / Geneva and Baden-Würtemburg / Alsace / Basel nexuses function this way. Globalization, decentralization, free trade agreements and instant communication have favoured this trend, which is further encouraged in Ontario's case by federal downsizing and offloading, by the Harris government's tax incentives and promotion of competitiveness, and by the province's location. Two-thirds of the Canadian consumer market and one-half of the American one are within one day's trucking distance of southern Ontario. Ontario's accelerating north-south integration into the North American economy will inevitably call for new administrative arrangements with its sister provinces and with the government in Ottawa.

Résumé

L'Ontario, qui a toujours été le "centre stratégique" du Canada, voit maintenant ce rôle historique évoluer en devenant plutôt un État-région de l'Amérique du Nord, c'est-à-dire un moteur économique caractérisé par son activité transfrontalière et son indépendance politique, économique et sociale de plus en plus marquée par rapport à l'État-nation dont elle est issue. C'est là un concept qui est déjà bien en place en Europe, où les axes Lyon / Turin / Genève et Baden-Würtemburg / Alsace / Bâle fonctionnent de la même manière. La mondialisation, la décentralisation, les accords de libre-échange et les communications instantanées ont favorisé cette tendance qui se trouve encore valorisée, dans le cas de l'Ontario, par les compressions et le délestage effectués par le palier fédéral, par les incitatifs fiscaux et la promotion de la compétitivité entrepris par le gouvernement Harris, de même que par la situation géographique de la province. Deux tiers du marché canadien et la moitié du marché nord-américain sont à moins d'une journée de camion du sud de l'Ontario. L'accélération de l'intégration de l'Ontario dans l'économie nord-américaine sur l'axe nord-sud exigera inéluctablement de nouveaux arrangements administratifs entre la province et ses consœurs, mais aussi avec le gouvernement central.

The principal dilemma of contemporary economic geography is the resurgence of regional economies and of territorial specialization in an age of increasing ease of transportation and communication (Storper, 1994, 22).

National Boundaries have become increasingly irrelevant in the definition of market and production spaces while regions, rather than countries, are emerging as key policy arenas (United Nations, 1990, iii).

On the global economic map, the lines that now matter are those defining what may be called "region states" (Ohmae, 1993, 78).

Introduction

The above visions of the emergence and role of region states provide the appropriate backdrop to this paper, the theme of which is that Ontario is evolving from its traditional role as Canadian "heartland" to its new geo-economic reality as a North American region state. Phrased differently, Ontario is fast becoming a heartland of North America. The purpose of the paper is to provide a descriptive-cum-analytical perspective of the emergence of this new Ontario and then to assess some of the implications for the operations of Canadian federalism.

The analysis in the first half of the paper proceeds by focusing on the constellation of influences—globalization and the knowledge/information revolution generally and, for Ontario, North American integration and fiscally-triggered decentralization—that are conspiring, as it were, to create region states. Within this general framework, section II (*Variations on the Region State*) defines the concept of region state, or economic nation state, for purposes of the ensuing analysis and, in particular, differentiates it from the more common concept of a political/ethnic region state or what Canadians refer to as a "distinct society". Section III, under the rubric of *Regional-International Interface*, then applies this vision of a sub-national region state to the European and Ontario geo-economies respectively. This largely descriptive approach to region state is followed by a more analytical perspective in Section IV (*Region States as the Embodiment of Untraded Interdependencies*) where, among other things, we attempt to make the case that the Harris government's Common Sense Revolution as well as the institutional/municipal revolutions can be viewed as an integral component of Ontario's shift towards a North-American-region-state status.

The second half of the paper effectively assumes that the Ontario region state is a fait accompli and directs attention to the range of implications for Ontario, for its sister provinces and for the federation. A brief conclusion completes the paper.

Variations on the Region State

A. DEFINING THE REGION STATE

We accept Kenichi Ohmae's (1995, 96) conception of region states, namely that they do not attempt "to solve all problems locally, but rather make it possible to solve them by *harnessing global resources* (emphasis added)." In principle, this implies that region states could lie either entirely within or across the borders of a nation state. For purposes of our analysis, however, we are (admittedly arbitrarily) linking region states with cross-border activity. For example, suppose that Manitoba geared its policies to penetrating the Ontario market and suppose, further, that it was wholly successful in this endeavour. From our perspective, Manitoba would not qualify as a region state because its entire focus is "inward", not international. Now we hasten to note that Manitoba might, in both principle and practice, be much better off gearing itself to the Ontario market than to the Minnesota (or US) market, but that is a quite separate issue from our perspective in this paper. In any event, this is hardly a restrictive assumption for Ontario since its "natural economic region" is cross-border, i.e., Ontario is, economically, progressively integrated into the Great Lakes basin.

While we are making an international reach a necessary condition for region-state status, it is not sufficient. Ontario was fully integrated into the North American automobile market during the Robarts mandate. Yet Ontario remained *heartland* in this era. Sufficiency requires that the political/administrative arsenal of the province/region also be deployed in a way that, simultaneously, pursues export penetration and embraces fully the global economy (Ohmae, 1995, 62). In other words, we are assuming that a region state be an active player in what we refer to as a "regional/international interface." And linkages between the region and the international economy must involve more than trading relationships.

There is a third characteristic advanced by Ohmae for a region state, namely that it be the right size and scale to be a "natural business unit" (1995, 5) in today's global economy. If one were to apply a strict interpretation to this, one might end up with a definition of Ontario's economic region that would be limited to the "golden horseshoe," and not the horseshoe plus eastern and northern Ontario. For some purposes, such as isolating North America's horizontally and vertically integrated industrial regions, this may well be the preferred definition. But not for our purposes which, given the federalism/governance focus, requires that the region state also be synchronous with sub-national administrative and political decision-making authority. We recognize that this assumption/definition will not find favour in all quarters.

Thus far, the above conditions have been of the "pull" variety—the potential region state is drawn rather naturally into the international arena or, to draw upon the language introduced earlier, is engaged in a regional-international interface. However, there can also be a powerful "push" factor emanating from the behaviour by central governments. To fall back once again on Ohmae (1995, 64): "in a borderless world, traditional national interest—which has become little more than a cloak for subsidy and protection—has no meaningful place." Thus, if the nation state attempts to give domestic subsidy and protection issues pride of policy place, as it were, this can serve as a powerful catalyst for sub-national governments to tilt their own policies in the direction of a region state. In the European environment, for example, the networking among Toulouse, Montpellier and Barcelona is motivated in part by the desire to escape from the policy frameworks of Paris and Madrid and to attempt to forge common ground for operating (and lobbying) under the European (Brussels) umbrella. More ominously, Ohmae (1995, 93) notes that "the marked inability [of central governments of nation states] to accept—or even acknowledge—global logic is slowly but surely dissolving the fabric holding nation states together". In the Canadian context, it is abundantly clear that Ottawa has not played its hand well from Ontario's vantage point. The discriminatory and fiscally damaging 1990 cap on the Canada Assistance Plan (CAP) (more recently rolled into the Canada Health and Social Transfer (CHST) entitlements), the financial impasse related to downloading training to Ontario, the favouring of Quebec over Ontario in terms of the allocation of federal immigration and refugee monies, the Finance Department's arbitrary pocketing of $7.1 billion (for 1997-98) of EI premiums (roughly 40% of which come from Ontario employers and employees), among other federal policies, have led successive Ontario administrations to come to believe that this federal discrimination is "systemic" (Courchene and Telmer, 1998, chapter 6 for Bob Rae's "fair share" federalism and chapter 8 for a similar Harris litany). By tilting its policy preferences toward east-west equity/distributional concerns relative to north-south allocative concerns, Ottawa is, in part at least, the author of Ontario's shift toward a region state.

With this bit of definitional backdrop, we are now in a position to survey some of the recent developments on the globalization and regional fronts as they relate to the political economy of Ontario's new role in the Canadian federation.

B. GLOCALIZATION AND DISTINCT SOCIETY

Globalization and the informatics revolution are transforming the nation state, especially the federal nation state. One need not go as far as Robert Reich (1991) and proclaim the death knell of the economic nation state, but we would align ourselves with Daniel Bell who, as far back as 1987, asserted that nation states had become too large to tackle the small things in life and too small to address the large things. Paquet (1995) refers to this as the "Gulliver Effect"—nation states are unable to deal effectively either with the dwarfs of Lilliput or the giants of Brobdingnag.

In terms of the erosion of the nation state "from above", as it were, the issue is straightforward: economic space is transcending political space, so that nation states are reacting, in countervailing fashion, by transferring important economic and regulatory powers to a supranational level. Examples are easy to come by—from the Bank for International Settlements imposition of capital-adequacy rules for global banks to the creation of supranational institutions like the EU and NAFTA.

The transfer of powers downward is less obvious, but not less important. One aspect of this is that the informatics revolution is dramatically enhancing "citizen power". We citizens now can access, send and otherwise manipulate information in ways and quantities that were undreamed of only a few short years ago and in ways that governments of all stripes are powerless to prevent. Indeed, in his global best-seller, *The Borderless World*, Ohmae (1990) actually defines globalization as "consumer sovereignty". Another aspect of the erosion of nation states from below is the transfer of powers to markets which, in turn, are inherently decentralizing. Yet another component of the downward transfer is highlighted by Horsman and Marshall (1995, xv):

> As the diminution of single-state power becomes evident, and as embryonic supranational political arrangements come only slowly into being, citizens will tend to think more closely ... about their own communities (variously defined ...), seeking local political reflections of their concerns, even as the economies in which they are consumers move even closer toward global integration. They will seek political solutions, and democratic accountability, at ever more local levels as the world economy moves toward an even greater level of integration.

This tendency for economic power to shift both to the global and local level is captured by the term "glocalization".

One result of this transfer of powers upward and downward from nation states is what Drucker (1986) refers to as the intriguing coincidence of an *integrating global economy* and a *splintering global polity*. Specifically, with the emergence of a supranational infrastructure (whether in terms of trade agreements, of a single market à la Europe 1992, or of the proposed common currency under Maastricht), sub-national units can leapfrog their national governments and tie themselves to these overarching structures.

Those sub-national units that are typically viewed as potential region states tend to combine the impacts of glocalization with one or more aspects of linguistic or socio-cultural distinctiveness. Hence, most analysts would view Catalonia as the leading exemplar of this type of region state—an economic powerhouse centred around Barcelona with substantial outward linkages, considerable and growing regional powers and a distinctive language and culture. And some might put Quebec in this category as well: it is culturally, linguistically and institutionally (e.g., civil law rather than common law), distinct and has much more in the way of political autonomy than Catalonia, but it is much less of an economic power, both domestic and internationally. In terms of other federal nations, Belgium would come to mind. The decentralized Belgian provinces appear to be latching on to the EU infrastructures, effectively eclipsing the traditional role for their federal government. And in recent years, both the richer Flemish province and the poorer Walloon province have been veering, willy-nilly, in the direction of becoming separate nation states. Where this would leave bilingual Brussels (the third of the three Belgian provinces and nestled in the Flemish region) is not entirely clear—perhaps as a European capital district. In any event, the Belgian cleavages are linguistic, although economic factors are also prominent.

While this association of region states with socio-cultural-linguistic distinctiveness is obviously important for some purposes (e.g., predicting which sub-national units may one day become sovereign nation states), it has minimal application to the case for Ontario as an emerging region state. Ontarians, by and large, share the same values as the rest of Canadians. Hence, the rationale for viewing Ontario as an emerging region state does not derive from any notion that the province is in any way a distinct society, at least in the traditional meaning of this term.

Nonetheless, the glocalization phenomenon remains relevant. With policies previously provided by Ottawa now coming under the rubric of GATT/WTO, or NAFTA or the Bank for International Settlements, the federal government matters less in these areas. And with earlier-noted transfer of powers downward in the federation, Queen's Park plays a much larger role in the way in which Ontarians live and work and play than heretofore was the case. In this sense, the new economic order is certainly a necessary condition to any conception of Ontario as a region state. Of and by itself, however, at best this would suggest that Ontario would become a highly decentralized province, not a region state.

Phrased differently, we need a different conception of a region state, one that does not depend on socio-cultural-linguistic distinctiveness. Enter the European regional science literature.

The Regional-International Interface

A. EUROPE

The European policy literature, especially the regional science literature, is well ahead of its North American counterpart in recognizing the increasing role played by cross-border regions. In part, this is because most of the powerful industrial regions have economic hinterlands that extend beyond national borders. Consider the Lyon (France), Turin (Italy) and Geneva (Switzerland) nexus:

> The Rhône-Alpes is France's strongest region, and Lyon, its capital and France's second-largest city, is a major international centre. Lyon's commercial policy is gaining independence and extending its European and global reach. Its airport was the first in France to acquire a high-speed rail link. Lyon's plan for growth includes high-speed rail service to Turin, Italy, which will require tunnelling 35 miles through the Alps but will cut travel time between the cities to just over an hour. The wealthy triangle formed by Lyon, Turin and Geneva—known as the Alpine Diamond—has a synergy that few regions of the world can match" (Newhouse, 1997, 71-72).

As a result of these and other major cross-border regions, there is a growing realization in policy circles that the traditional *national-national interface* is giving way to a *regional-international interface*. Newhouse (1997, 67) notes that two parallel and related processes have emerged: "One is regionalism, the other globalization: instead of working through national capitals, European regions are linking themselves directly to the global economy" and, further (p. 69), "in this more freewheeling environment, bankers and industrial planners have begun to view Europe at least as much as a group of distinct economic regions as an assortment of nation states."

A second implication is the recognition that comparative advantage is largely a regional rather than a national phenomenon. The obvious corollary is particularly important:

"regionalism is much more than a return to cultural roots or a distancing from national capitals. It has as much to do with wealth creation as anything else" (Newhouse, 1997, 69).

That this resonates well with what is emerging in Ontario will be the focus of much of the rest of this paper. In the remainder of the present section, we shall continue with European examples.

From the Ontario perspective, the best known example of the regional-international interface is the 1988 "Four Motors Association". The four participants were the regions surrounding Stuttgart (Baden-Würtemberg), Barcelona (Catalonia), Lyon (Rhône-Alpes), and Milan (Lombardy). (In 1989, Ontario became an "associate" member of the Four Motors Association, an indication that the concept of cross-border regionalism was wholly familiar to the Peterson Liberals). In many areas, these four regions have more in common with each other than with other regions of their respective countries. Thus, the agreement serves as a template for coordinating their common industrial and cross-border interests and it also serves to coordinate and enhance their lobbying efforts and influence with Brussels (i.e., with the EU).

These and other efforts in the direction of embracing the regional-international interface raise a potentially difficult problem for Europe and one with direct carry-over to Ontario and Canada. In Newhouse's (1997, 72-73) words:

If the larger purpose of the Four Motors Association is wealth creation rather than a conscious return to roots, will the process drive politics in its and other regions to the right, especially as some become richer and others poorer? And who will protect the poor and disadvantaged? Nation States? The EU?

Carried over to the Ontario setting, this has potentially dramatic implications for Canadian federalism. At one extreme is a centre-driven policy which props up the poorer regions at the expense of the richer regions. This implies active intervention in the allocation, east-west, of economic activity. The other is to allow the richer regions to pursue wealth creation as they see fit. Ottawa would then come in as an active intervenor on the distributional front. Actually, this may not be the other extreme, since it assumes the continued adherence on the part of Canadians to a "sharing community". If this adherence erodes, then the other polar solution may involve no federal intervention on either the allocation or distribution front and the acceptance of greater disparities across provinces. One implication of the emergence of Ontario as a region state is that we will not have the luxury of ignoring this daunting policy challenge. More on this later.

In other aspects, the European situation does not (at least as yet) have a direct carry-over to Ontario. For example, Baden-Würtemberg (Germany), Alsace (France) and Basel (Switzerland) are now one region for employment purposes (Newhouse, 1997, 71). The FTA and NAFTA provide for free movement of goods and services, but not of people. For how long can this be sustained? How long will it be before Ontario attempts to engage in sectoral agreements providing for much greater cross-border labour mobility?

This brings us to our final European example:

"What is clear is that in this age of global trade and capital flows, not to mention information highways and high-speed travel, local entities feel better placed to manage their affairs than distant bureaucracies whether in national capitals or in Brussels. The German state of Baden-Würtemberg, for example, is making its own foreign and trade policies; it has signed several hundred agreements with other regions and entities" (Newhouse, 1997, 68-69).

Now the relationship between Baden-Würtemberg and Bonn (or Berlin) is quite different from that between Ontario and Ottawa. One key difference is that the German upper chamber (Bundesrat) is comprised of delegates from the Länder (i.e., the provinces, in our terms). Moreover, negotiations relating to international agreements involving the constitutional competences of the Länder are handled by the Bundesrat. This differs radically from the Canadian reality. However, Ontario has much more in the way of legislative and policy freedom than does Baden-Würtemberg, i.e., Canada is much more decentralized than is Germany.

Therefore, unlike many other potential region states (Lyon, Milan, etc.) Ontario not only has the economic/industrial power and the cross-border economic hinterland, but it also has a degree of political/administrative power that *no* European region can match. And all of these aspects of Ontario's potential as a region state are now coming into play.

With this European backdrop, we now direct our focus on Ontario.

B. ONTARIO

1. Ontario As a North American Economic Force

We now turn to the pre-eminent driving force behind the new Ontario—its economic relationship within North America. Appendix 9A of Courchene and Telmer (1998) details selected salient features of the Ontario economy in the broader North American context, features that relate to location, trade, economic strengths, industrial penetration, workforce characteristics and miscellaneous attributes. What emerges is not only that Ontario is strategically positioned within the North American market but, as well, that the province is a veritable economic powerhouse within this North American environment. For example:

- Two-thirds of the Canadian consumer market (about 18 million people) and half of the US consumer market (about 125 million people) are within one day's trucking of southern Ontario. The corresponding disposable income in this market (for 1993) exceeds US $2 trillion, with retail sales exceeding US $1 trillion. Ontario's consumer markets are larger than many US counterparts, e.g., household income within 400 miles of Toronto is as high or greater than it is for Cleveland, Detroit, Boston and New York.

- In terms of industrial reach, three quarters of Canadian manufacturing firms and over half of all US manufacturing firms are within a day's trucking of southern Ontario.

- Ontario is an especially desirable location for reaching certain industrial markets: for example, Ontario accounts for 96% of materials and supplies used in Canada's motor vehicles and parts industries, 71% in the scientific and professional equipment sector. In terms of industrial reach, 66.9% of the Canada/US printing and publishing industry, 60.1% of rubber and plastics, 67.8% of primary metals and 67.6% of transportation equipment lies within a day's shipping of Ontario.

It is these and other locational/economic/industrial features that underpin Ontario's shift in focus from east-west trade to north-south trade.
We now focus in more detail on this shift in trade patterns.

2. North-South vs East-West Trade

Chart 1 presents a dramatic picture of Ontario's rapidly rising North American economic integration. From a 1981 base where Ontario's exports to the rest of the world (ROW) and its exports to the other provinces (ROC) were roughly equal at $40 billion, by 1995 international exports had soared to about $140 billion, now roughly two and a half times the level of ROC exports. While the ROW data includes exports to all countries, Ontario's exports are predominantly to the US and the proportion of US to total Ontario exports has actually increased over this period.

Chart 1 – Ontario Trade

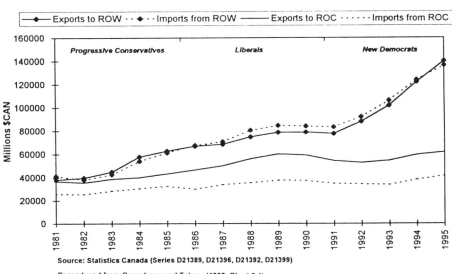

Source: Statistics Canada (Series D21389, D21396, D21392, D21399)

Reproduced from Courchene and Telmer (1998, Chart 9.1)

Table 1 provides further detail on the ROW-ROC split by province. In 1981, six provinces exported more to the rest of Canada than to the rest of the world (i.e., the 1981 value of the ratio, ROW/ROC, in column 3 is less than unity for six provinces). Only Newfoundland, New Brunswick, Saskatchewan and B.C. exported more to the rest of the world in 1981 than to the other provinces. The Ontario data in Table 1 for 1981 reveal rough equality for ROW and ROC exports.

Table 1: Interprovincial and International Trade (goods and services, 1986$)

	EXPORTS			IMPORTS			TRADE BALANCE			E/GDP
	ROC	ROW	ROW/ ROC	ROC	ROW	ROW/ ROC	ROC	ROW	Total	(Col 1 + Col2)/GDP
	(1)	(2)	(3)	(4)	(5)	(6)	(7)	(8)	(9)	(10)
CANADA										
1981	116.58	101.85	.87	116.58	105.3	.90	0.0	3.45	3.45	.49
1994	133.98	225.82	1.68	133.98	229.10	1.71	0.0	-3.28	-3.28	.60
NFLD										
1981	.85	1.98	2.33	3.32	.97	.29	-2.47	1.01	-2.46	.47
1994	1.13	2.01	1.78	3.55	1.92	.54	-2.42	.09	-2.33	.43
PEI										
1981	.50	.19	.38	.87	.15	.17	-.37	.04	-.33	.56
1994	.69	.32	.46	1.07	.31	.29	-.38	.01	-.37	.52
NS										
1981										
1994	2.97	1.81	.61	5.00	3.02	.60	-2.03	-1.21	-3.24	.44
	3.15	3.45	1.10	5.56	4.56	.82	-2.41	-1.11	-3.52	.44
NB										
1981										
1994	2.31	2.47	1.07	4.05	2.48	.61	-1.74	-.01	-1.75	.59
	3.70	3.73	1.01	5.02	4.06	.81	-1.32	-.33	-1.65	.62
QC										
1981	27.60	21.94	.79	24.13	23.51	.97	3.47	-1.57	1.90	.47
1994	29.49	41.62	1.41	28.13	47.93	1.71	1.36	-6.31	-4.95	.53
ONT										
1981	47.04	45.07	.96	30.00	47.76	1.57	17.04	-2.69	14.35	.54
1994	54.05	113.59	2.10	34.50	124.31	3.60	19.55	-10.72	8.83	.70
MAN										
1981	5.11	2.65	.52	6.37	2.75	.43	-1.26	-.10	-1.36	.49
1994	5.30	6.00	1.13	7.14	5.60	.78	-1.84	.40	-1.44	.58
SASK										
1981	3.55	4.21	1.19	7.84	2.96	.38	-4.29	1.25	-3.04	.52
1994	5.53	7.00	1.27	8.58	3.61	.42	-3.05	3.39	.34	.66
AB										
1981	18.20	9.01	.50	19.31	11.28	.58	-1.11	-2.27	-3.38	.51
1994	19.54	25.42	1.30	20.75	14.65	.71	-1.21	10.67	9.46	.63
BC										
1981	8.21	12.51	1.52	13.45	9.27	.74	-5.24	3.24	-2.00	.38
1994	10.64	22.06	2.07	17.69	21.22	1.20	-7.05	.84	-6.21	.44

Source: *Provincial Economic Accounts, Annual Estimates: 1981-94*, Table 3.
Reproduced from Courchene and Telmer (1998, Table 9.1)

However, by 1994, only PEI exported more to ROC than to the rest of the world. Ontario now leads the way in terms of international export penetration with a ROW/ROC ratio of 2.10 (column 3 of Table 9.1 for 1994), with B.C. a close second. More recent data (Crane, 1997) comparing 1990 and 1995 for Ontario indicate that Ontario's ROW exports have grown over this 1990-1995 period nearly eight times as fast as export to the rest of Canada. If this trend continues, even if it continues at, say, four rather than eight times the rate of east-west export expansion, the pressures to focus *all* energies north-south will be overwhelming. If, in the European context, Newhouse (1997, 68) can proclaim that "regionalism, whether within or across national borders, is Europe's current and future dynamic", then this holds with even more force in Canada (and particularly in Ontario) with the important proviso that our regional dynamics are unmistakably cross-border.

As an important analytical aside, recent research by McCallum (1995), Helliwell (1996), and Helliwell and McCallum (1995) has demonstrated that, corrected for population size and distance (via the traditional gravity model) internal trade is roughly 20 times more than cross-border trade. Thus, borders *do* matter in the sense that the internal Canadian economic union is much more integrated than the cross-border economic union. This should not come as a surprise. Apart from the fact that the very intent of the 1879 National Policy was to privilege east-west trade rather than north-south trade, a key factor is the high degree of legal, institutional and social *comity* that prevails within Canada. Hartt (1992, 5) defines the principle of comity as "reciprocal courtesy extended by one jurisdiction to another in friendly recognition of each other's laws" which, in turn, "oil the wheels of commerce" and then adds (14):

> The least-noticed aspect of the [Canadian] economic union is not mandated by the Constitution at all, but results instead from a myriad of laws based on comity among provinces. These courtesy laws enable individuals and firms that conduct business in one province to enjoy a favoured status in other provinces in relation to such matters as obtaining licenses to carry on business, having a standing in the courts for legal actions, registering security interests against prosperity, enforcing judgements, and like matters that function as the workaday tools of economic man ... Canadians have advanced, established rules about such things, but, above all they enjoy a system that affords advantages to all those partaking in the economic union called Canada.

What the data in Chart 1 and Table 1 indicate is that, despite the higher degree of economic integration in the Canadian market, the sheer size of the US market is now dominating trade flows. And these trade flows, especially to the US, will continue to grow. Indeed, the FTA and NAFTA are best viewed not as agreements for removing trade barriers but, rather, as instruments that attempt to establish cross-border relationships that, in effect, increase "comity". What this means is that the 20-to-1 ratio reported in the Helliwell-McCallum research will begin to fall sharply. Even if the ratio were to fall only to 10-to-1, this would imply a doubling of international exports in Chart 1.

When these emerging trading patterns are viewed in tandem with the locational and economic/industrial characteristics of Ontario alluded to above, the appeal of a North American economic focus becomes fully evident. In terms of the "one day's trucking" referred to earlier, if one assumes that the Canadian component of this includes Quebec and Manitoba, then the US "one day's trucking" market is seventeen times as large as the Canadian component. Small wonder, then, that Ontario's economic future lies in middle America. This is the fundamental economic reality underpinning the new Ontario, and short of US moves to the contrary, the emerging trade patterns are not only irreversible, but will intensify.

It is important to note that while this shifting of Ontario's focus north-south relates to what one would call "trade determinism" or "economic determinism", there is more at play here: it also reflects an important degree of "institutional determinism", namely the FTA and NAFTA. Specifically, with progressively porous borders and with principles such as national treatment, a failure by Ontario to pursue aggressively its interests within North America could easily result in a cross-border movement of key aspects of its economic base.

However, Ontario's huge and increasing regional-international interface does not translate directly into the province becoming a North American region state. What this requires is that Queen's Park becomes the focus for preserving, promoting and enhancing the province's economic future within North America. It is within this context that Ottawa's recent policies with respect to the provinces (and especially with respect to Ontario) take on a wholly different interpretation—by effectively abandoning the "heartland" across a wide range of policies (the cap on CAP, the CHST, training, EI, immigration, etc.), Ottawa has literally forced Ontario to assume a much more prominent role in safeguarding its economic position within Canada and North America. Moreover, this process is likely to be characterized by positive feedbacks. Once Ontario begins to operate in more policy areas, citizens will call upon the province to begin operating in adjacent areas. In other words, the relevance of the province to Ontarians will become larger. Beyond this, Ontarians, traditionally the most unhyphenated of Canadians, are by virtue of federal devolution and offloading being invited, if not encouraged, to henceforth seek out aspects of their "identity" in Queen's Park rather than Parliament Hill. How else would one describe the financial offloading of medicare to Queen's Park and the provinces, generally. And, as will be elaborated later, the provinces are responding by articulating pan-Canadian principles and processes toward this end.

Thus, if the mushrooming north-south trade has provided the "pull" factor underpinning Ontario's transition toward a region state, Ottawa provided the needed "push". This is ironical since it was overall federal macro policy (FTA/NAFTA, monetary policy, deficit reduction and the GST) that paved the way for Ontario to become more competitive in the North American context.

In any event, Ontario is now a North American region state.

Prior to focusing on the implications for the province and for Canada that flow from Ontario's region-state status, we shall devote some attention to the analytical underpinnings of the concept of a region state.

Region States as Embodiments of Untraded Interdependencies

It is much more difficult to sort out the analytics relating to region states than to document their empirical existence. In general, the relevant literature (most of it European) falls into the "evolutionary" economics school rather than the neoclassical school. Specifically, the emphasis is not on equilibria (as it would be if the analysis were neoclassical), but on innovation, on agents of change, and on the role of institutional and structural elements. Indeed, the emphasis on path-dependency, on feedback mechanisms and on irreversibilities is central to this literature and predates the appearance of these concepts in mainstream economies as reflected, for example, in the recent literature on endogenous growth.

One important strand of this rich regional literature relates to the role of *local milieux* in generating networking which, in turn, can be characterized by organizational principles and linkages that encourage flexibility, the creation and transmission of knowledge, skill formation, mutual trust among partners, and so on (Lecoq, 1991, 239). Thus, these "milieux innovateurs" are, at the same time, *organizational* (in the sense that they embody a set of institutions, rules, conventions and practices) and *territorial* (in the sense that they are embedded in the social and economic infrastructure of the region).

Geographer Michael Storper (1994) extends this analysis by postulating that the success of Silicon Valley, Route 128 and other industrial "hot spots" must reside in what he calls *untraded interdependencies*. The "untraded" aspect is critical, since it implies that to access these interdependencies one must be located in the regional economy:

> Thus, regional economies constitute the nexus of untraded interdependencies which emerge and become, themselves, specific but public assets of production communities (assets of coordination, i.e., frameworks of collective action), and which underpin the production and reproduction of other specific assets such as labour and hardware (1994, 21).

One could, and probably should, expand this definition to explicitly include assets like social capital, although they are probably implicitly included. Economists may have a difficult time grappling with these concepts because their discipline is inherently market (i.e., tradeables) based. Hence, their focus is typically on "traded interdependencies" which, by definition, are not location specific. As a result, mainstream economists have not, until recently, played a major role in the development of this literature.

An alternative way to conceive of these untraded interdependencies is to view them as "locational externalities", hopefully *positive* locational externalities but they could obviously be negative as well. One could conceive of a series of these externalities—one might relate to the interdependencies at the industry/production level, another could involve the forward and backward linkages among education/training, income support and labour and product markets and a third might involve the set of public goods. Focusing on the third of these, a firm locating anywhere in North America has access to an international public good—NAFTA. If, among Canada, the US and Mexico, the firm chooses to locate in Canada, it gains access to Canadian public goods (such as medicare for its workers) but foregoes access to the comparable US and Mexican national public goods and/or infrastructures. And if the firm locates in Ontario, it acquires the Ontario set, not the Alberta or Quebec set, of provincial public goods. Because we have focused our example on public goods, it is fairly easy to see that they are inherently untradeable—one accesses them by location, not by markets (although one could in some cases use markets to attempt to replicate another jurisdiction's public goods, e.g., a firm in the US could provide medicare for its workers). Indeed, one might extend Storper's conception by suggesting that the process of competitive federalism can be viewed as an attempt among sub-national units to compete with each other in the provision of these untraded interdependencies or positive locational externalities. The new twist, drawing from the emerging regional-international interface, is that this competition is no longer along east-west (interprovincial) lines but along cross-border (international) lines.

The above analysis is admittedly tentative and incomplete. The literature on networking and externalities in light of internationalization and the informatics revolution is literally exploding. Indeed, one could probably come at the concept of a region state entirely from a networking framework. For example, sociologist Manuel Castells in his sure-to-be classic *The Rise of the Network Society* (1996) offers the following assessment of the implications of globalization and the informatics revolution:

> The global economy emerging from information-based production and competition is characterized by its *interdependence*, its *asymmetry*, its *regionalization*, the *increasing diversification within each region*, its *selective inclusiveness*, its *exclusionary segmentation*, and, as a result of all these features, an extraordinarily *variable geometry* that tends to dissolve historical economic geography (p. 106, emphasis in original).

This is fully consistent with our own views of the supplanting of the traditional national-national relationship with the regional-international interface and the emergence of the region state.

A. ONTARIO AND UNTRADED INTERDEPENDENCIES

While the evolution of Ontario toward region state status began well before the Harris government came on the scene, it is nonetheless the case that the Ontario of neither Peterson nor Rae would qualify as a region state in terms of the definition we developed above. For example, the Peterson Liberals never did buy into the FTA, at least not officially. Nor did Rae's NDP buy into the FTA or NAFTA. And neither premier accepted the rationale underpinning the GST, namely its export/import neutrality and, therefore, its inherent resonance with the concept of a North American region state. Beyond this, one can easily make a case that in terms of attracting foreign investment, Peterson and especially Rae were engaged in creating *negative* locational externalities—Peterson by embarking on an incredible spending spree that left Ontario among the high-tax, high-transfer provinces in Canada (and especially in North America) and Rae by doubling the province's indebtedness and triggering successive decreases in its credit ratings.

With the Harris government, all of this changed. Ontario bought into the full range of federal policies designed to promote export penetration and competitiveness. Moreover, by setting the province's fiscal house in order, including cuts in personal income taxation, the Conservatives have certainly made Ontario a more attractive business location within North America. Beyond this, we would suggest that the ongoing institutional/municipal revolution ought to be considered as an integral part of creating untraded interdependencies or positive locational externalities.

On the latter point, the underlying issue can be best addressed in terms of Chart 2. The solid line in Chart 2 depicts Ontario unit labour costs in Canadian dollars while the dotted line traces US unit labour costs in US dollars. Both series are arbitrarily set at 1.00 in 1980. These unit labour costs are a combination of wage inflation (which increases unit labour costs) and productivity growth (which decreases them). The dashed line presents Ontario's unit labour costs in US dollars. If the comparison is made between US and Ontario unit labour costs (ULCs) where both are expressed in US dollars (that is, if the comparison is between the dotted line and the dashed line), Ontario is considerably more competitive in 1995, vis-à-vis the US, than it was in 1980. In turn, this reflects primarily the depreciation in the Canadian dollar from its near 90 US cent level in 1991 to the current low-70-cent level. Over the longer term, however, the key to maintaining an advantageous ULC performance in Ontario is to ensure that Ontario wage inflation does not outpace US wage inflation and that Ontario productivity increases apace with US productivity. As a result of the Bank of Canada's 1988 shift toward price inflation, Canada and Ontario have performed well on the wage inflation front. But, we still lag behind the Americans in terms of productivity increases. In this context, the traumatic industrial restructuring of Ontario's manufacturing sector during the 1990s recession went a considerable distance toward closing the productivity gap in the private sector. As noted in Appendix 9A of Courchene and Telmer (1998), manufacturing productivity in Ontario increased at an annual rate of 4.4% over 1991-94 and is on course for a smaller, but nonetheless healthy, 3.3% increase from 1995 to 1998. However, with close to 50% of the Ontario economy not subject to market clearing mechanisms, Ontario is behind the eight ball in closing the productivity gap vis-à-vis the American model unless it addresses public sector productivity. While not downplaying the Conservatives' ideological bent in terms of this exercise, the untraded-interdependencies framework provides an *analytical* perspective for the municipal/institutional revolution, namely to increase productivity in the public sector and, thereby, to enhance Ontario's locational positive externalities within the North American market. Note that this does not represent a claim on our part that the ongoing restructuring of the public sector *will* increase productivity. It is far too soon to tell whether or not this will be the case. Rather, our claim is that public sector productivity must increase if Ontario is to become an effective North American region state. The current focus on whether or not this restructuring will result in immediate savings is not the key issue, since productivity improvements are likely to take time to be realized. Admittedly, this makes the municipal/institutional revolution a difficult exercise politically, since the costs are immediate and personalized across the population whereas the benefits, should they occur, will be both delayed and diffuse.

Chart 2 – Unit Labour Costs (Manufacturing)
Unit labour costs are defined as labour compensation divided by real GDP

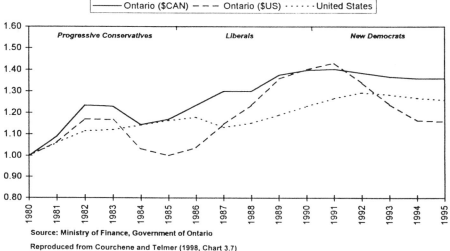

Source: Ministry of Finance, Government of Ontario

Reproduced from Courchene and Telmer (1998, Chart 3.7)

In this context, the very recent (August 1997) Ontario hydro debacle presents a special challenge. Even prior to the report that triggered the mothballing of several nuclear reactors, Hydro was under considerable competitive pressures arising from the US deregulation of its energy sector. Actually, this institutional meltdown of Hydro presents the Harris government with a great opportunity to deregulate electricity—a liberalized

market for electricity would have a significant impact on the future economic health of the province. It would be a major mistake on the part of the
Conservatives if they did not tackle Hydro restructuring during their current mandate.

At this juncture, it might appear that we are equating the notion of a region state and positive locational externalities with the existence of
laissez-faire capitalism. This is not the case. Region states can be expo-
nents of either communitarian or individualist capitalism and they can be
high-transfer or low-transfer economies. The confusion arises, in part at
least, because the Harris government inherited a fiscal crisis and it had to
sort this out in the context of privileging Ontario and Ontarians in the North
American context. What fiscal flexibility the government has achieved has
been deployed not to accelerate deficit reduction or the reduction in personal income tax rates, but to enhance the human-capital/innovation nexus
as reflected in the 1997 Ontario budget (and elaborated in Chapter 7 of
Courchene and Telmer, 1998). Our view is that if and when the Harris government is voted out of office, the successor government will in all likelihood not pull back on the salient elements that have contributed to Ontario's increasing competitive advantage in North American markets.

The key point is that Ontario's traditional "heartland" role in the Canadian federation has been overwhelmed. But with what implications for the
province and the federation?

Ontario as a Region State: Implications

In the conclusion of *What Does Ontario Want?* Courchene (1989, 45)
notes:

> Ontario's power and influence *will* be exercised within the
> federation in one way or another. A central government
> conforming more to a confederal than a federal mould will surely
> tend to ensure that Ontarians begin progressively to articulate their
> interests through Queen's Park (and with a different agenda!). For
> example, the on-going controversy between Ottawa and Ontario as
> to whether the province can levy a "flat tax" would effectively be
> solved by Ontario implementing its own personal income tax.
> Phrased differently, if the federal government comes to be
> perceived by Ontarians as not adequately reflecting the interests of
> Ontario, the end result will be a much stronger Queen's Park, a
> much more decentralized federation and by definition, a much
> weaker central government. While this is diametrically opposed to

Ontario's [traditional] preferred conception of the federation, it is
nonetheless an eminently viable alternative for the province and,
as such, ought to give all federal politicians all kinds of pause for
thought. Moreover, even some of the "province rights" provinces
would have second thoughts about this scenario.

Although penned nearly a decade ago, this scenario is now upon us.
We are witnessing a much stronger Queen's Park, a much more decentralized federation and a much weaker central government (and the above reference to a separate personal income tax (PIT) for Ontario is certainly apt,
given that the 1997 Ontario budget has raised the possibility that Ontario
will mount its own, separate PIT). But these changes are not merely cast in
the largely political framework envisaged in the above quotation: they also,
and primarily, are embedded in the emerging geo-economic reality of
North America. The result is that the province of Ontario is now a region
state or, perhaps even more apt, an "economic nation state".

The key implication of Ontario as a region state or an economic nation
state is that the province now is engaged in policies and processes that are
designed to enhance the ability of Ontarians and Ontario to compete within
the North American and global market place. What makes this such a
daunting challenge for the federation is that Ontario's desire for additional
powers to create these positive untraded interdependencies is not about
"beggar thy neighbour" federalism. Nor is it about extracting greater powers from Ottawa for their own sake. Rather it is, as noted, about favourably
positioning Ontario and Ontarians vis-à-vis its competitors, which tend to
be less and less its sister provinces. And the fact that British Columbia and
Quebec (and perhaps Alberta) have demands that are similarly conceived
makes Ottawa's role all the more complex.

Moreover, Ottawa's policies are also profoundly affected by globalization and enhanced North American integration. As Keating (1994, 3)
points out, rather than allocate resources to backward regions, nations increasingly will feel compelled to favour their most dynamic sectors and lo-
cations to maximize national competitiveness and, therefore, to enhance
the probability of attracting transnational-enterprise capital. Phrased differently, the opportunity cost of federally-driven, interventionist regional
policy is, increasingly, international competitiveness. While this may be
viewed as an appropriate and long overdue policy shift (and one that will
rest well with Ontario as a region state), it does alter existing regional-
national linkages and identities. In the face of this integration-triggered
shift to economic liberalism on the allocative front, how does Ottawa respond to the resulting distributional concerns of the provinces, particularly

the have-not provinces? Conceptually, one obvious answer would be for Ottawa to play a larger role in the delivery of some of the public goods and services that define us as Canadians (e.g., medicare, welfare, post-secondary education). In reality, however, not only are these areas largely under provincial control, but Ottawa has been sharply curtailing its role here, except perhaps for welfare in light of the 1997 budget provision for an enriched child tax benefit.

This child-tax-credit initiative in the 1997 federal budget probably merits special highlight since it can be given a rationale in the context of the emergence of region states. Earlier we noted that the policies followed by the "four motors" of continental Europe (Rhône-Alpes, Baden Würtemberg, Lombardy and Catalonia) were driven by wealth creation and tended to incorporate the politics of the "right". The issue then becomes: who will protect the poor and disadvantaged of less affluent regions? This focus on wealth creation or on allocative efficiency is obviously driving Harris's Ontario. Is Ontario's apparent willingness (apparent, because the details of the provincial side of the child-benefit initiatives have not been finalized) to buy into this scheme a portent for the future—Ontario pushes an allocative rather than a redistributive agenda which then spurs Ottawa to act on the redistributive front (in this case, the national child benefit) which then makes it easier for Ontario to continue to pursue or even intensify its allocative or wealth-creation thrust. Indeed, one can mount a fairly convincing case that the federal government's role in social Canada should be to play the key role for the children and the elderly, which will then leave the provinces to integrate the adults into a comprehensive human capital subsystem. However, in the above scenario this comes about because region states are privileging allocation over redistribution.

There is, however, a potential downward spiral that could be set in motion here, unless Ottawa plays its cards right. If, for example, the federal government responds to the claims of lagging regions by introducing policies that discriminate with respect to individuals on the basis of province of residence, then the "have" provinces will react, rationally and appropriately, by pressing for a further devolution of powers and by pursuing wealth creation to a heightened degree. Ottawa would be well advised to keep its pro-poor-province/region initiatives *within* the equalization program and to ensure that any policies directed toward individuals are "blind" to province of residence. If not, then the support for the equalization program itself will begin to erode.

Some elaboration is warranted here. Students of Canadian social policy and federalism would no doubt agree that for much of the post-war period Ontario and Ontarians were more supportive of the east-west transfer system than were Albertans or British Columbians (or at least than were their governments). Public choice analysts would probably not attribute this to any inherent "generosity" or altruism on the part of Ontarians as compared with residents of BC or Alberta. Rather, their argument would be that the "second-round" spending impacts of these transfers tended to end up somewhere in Ontario, since trade largely flowed east-west and Ontario was the principal north-south conduit. With generalized north-south trade (as reflected in Table 1 data), however, these second-round spending impacts may now end up in North Carolina or Minnesota and not in Ontario. This could well serve to alter the distributional tastes of Ontarians *even with unchanged attitudes to east-west distribution* because the economic cost to Ontarians of these transfers has now increased. Might Ontarians' tastes for east-west redistribution tend towards those of BC and Alberta, where there was never any expectation that they would be the recipients of any second-round spending impacts? The public choice answer would be in the affirmative.

A. REGIONAL ECONOMIC DIVERSITY

It is not just that nearly all Canada's provinces are more integrated (in terms of the exports) internationally than east-west, but also that Canada's regions, which in some cases would incorporate more than one province, are economically/industrially quite distinct from one another. As already noted, this means that it is time to view Canada as a series of north-south, cross-border economies with quite distinct industrial structures. British Columbia is oriented toward the Pacific Rim and the US Northwest; the energy-based Alberta economy competes with the oil and gas producing regions of the Texas Gulf; the breadbaskets of Saskatchewan and Manitoba keep a competitive watch on the US midwest; the Great Lakes economies of Ontario and Quebec are integrated with each other and with their counterparts south of the border; and the fortunes of Atlantic Canada likely will increasingly be linked to the Atlantic Rim and the Boston/New York axis. To this regional economic diversity we must add the information contained in Chart 3, namely that the business cycles in these diverse regions are not synchronous.

From the upper panel of Chart 3, four years after the onset of the 1980s recession, employment in Ontario was 105% of the pre-recession peak, whereas employment in Alberta and especially British Columbia was still well below the pre-recession peak. The 1990s recession was entirely different. British Columbia skated through the recession with nary a negative

Chart 3
Employment and Recovery after Two Recessions

A: 1980s Recession
Employment Recovered Four Years Later?

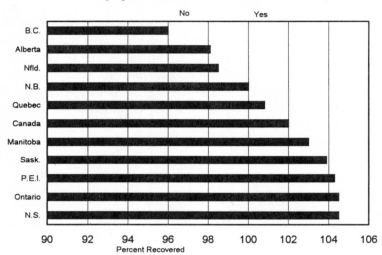

B: 1990s Recession
Employment Recovered Four Years Later?

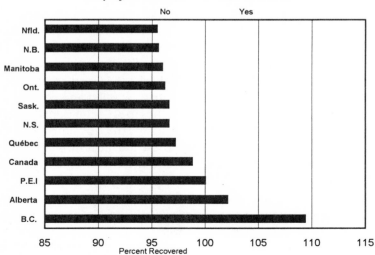

Sources: Statistics Canada, TD Bank, Department of Economic Research

Reproduced from Courchene and Telmer (1998, Chart 9.2)

impact—four years after the recession its employment was nearly 110% above the previous peak. In contrast, Ontario's employment was still well below its pre-recession high. This non-synchronization of regional economic cycles poses stabilization problems for our macro managers: there is only one monetary policy and only one exchange rate. Active pursuit of either as a stabilization instrument is apt to drag the policy authorities into the "politics" of regional fortunes.

Taken together, these geo-economic features of the upper half of North America (increasing north-south integration and the non-synchronization of business cycles) lead to some important observations. One of these is that the manner in which a Great Lakes economy might want to integrate apprenticeship, training, welfare, UI/EI, education and the transition to work will likely differ from the way a Pacific Rim economy like BC might like to forge this same integration. In turn, this means that Ottawa has to allow substantial policy flexibility at the provincial level or else the provinces (at least the "have" provinces and Quebec) will demand additional powers—for example, some provincial control over EI in order to make these benefits more integrated with the provincial welfare/training/apprenticeship subsystems. In any event, the economic diversity across Canada's regions also implies policy diversity, the common term for which is "asymmetry".

The second observation relates to a different type of asymmetry. Not all provinces will have the ability or the desire to "take down" the full range of powers that other provinces may want to accept or wrest from the federal government. In turn, this will lead to a further asymmetry across provinces. The only way in which the end result would not involve more asymmetry would be for some of the smaller provinces to exercise these powers in unison with their neighbouring provinces (as the three Atlantic provinces are doing in connection with the Harmonized Sales Tax). To be sure, the Canadian federation is already rife with asymmetries (Courchene 1995, 8) so that some additional asymmetry need not pose a problem. However, there may and likely will be a difference in that these new asymmetries will relate not to the traditional demands from Quebec for additional powers, but, rather, to the demands on the part of Ontario and likely the other "have" provinces. Indeed, Ontario in the millennium will likely be willing to exercise *more* powers than will Quebec. This will further complicate the already existing have vs. have-not province divide that Premier Savage (1996) so eloquently articulated.

The final observation in this context relates to the way that the federal government manages the combination of regional diversity and north-south integration. As north-south integration intensifies further, both in

terms of trade flows and even more importantly in terms of arrangements /
agreements covering trade, institutional, and legal issues, it will become
progressively more difficult for the provinces to tolerate abrupt shifts in the
Canadian / US exchange rate (except, perhaps, in the unlikely event of policy aberration on the part of the Americans). This need not involve abandoning flexible exchange rates as long as both monetary authorities are tar-
geting roughly the same inflation rate (Courchene, 1997). However, if this
shared view of the appropriate inflation target does not hold, then Ontario
as a region state will clearly argue for a fixed exchange rate (or at least
greater exchange-rate fixity than has characterized the last dozen years or
so) with its principal North American market.

B. AN ONTARIO PERSONAL INCOME TAX (PIT)?

In his 1997 budget, Ontario finance minister Ernie Eves raised the possibility that Ontario would implement its own, separate, PIT. While Eves's
rationale for such an initiative was couched in terms of rising dissatisfac-
tion, and even frustration, with the manner that Ottawa was and is
administering the Tax Collection Agreements, it is not difficult to make a
rather appealing case for an Ontario-run PIT in the context of its emergence
as a North American region state. We have addressed the costs and benefits
of an Ontario PIT elsewhere (Courchene and Telmer, 1998, chapter 8 and
Courchene, 1997a). For present purposes we shall restrict ourselves to two
observations.

The first draws from the implicit story contained in Charts 1 and 3,
namely Ontario's increasing north-south integration on the one hand and
the differing business cycle patterns across the provinces, which reflect the
different provincial economic structures, on the other. What this means is
that, increasingly, the jurisdictions that are important in terms of tax harmonization are no longer Ontario's sister provinces but progressively the
US Great Lakes states. For this purpose, Ontario's control over its share of
the PIT could become an effective new instrument in generating positive
locational externalities vis-à-vis its southern competitors. This, too, is what
a North American region state is all about.

The second observation follows directly from the first. One of the advantages of the existing Tax Collection Agreements is that they serve to
promote the internal fiscal and economic union. For example, provincial
tax credits that have the effect of fragmenting the economic union are disal-
lowed under the Agreements. A separate Ontario PIT would mean that the
province would no longer be so constrained, although one could fall back
on the internal market constitutional provisions to keep Ontario in line.

The larger point here is that our traditional approaches to managing the federation are being overwhelmed by globalization in general and by the emergence of Ontario as a region state in particular. Phrased differently, the federation is in need of some new processes and instrumentalities. Enter intergovernmentalism and the ACCESS model.

C. THE ACCESS MODEL

Chart 4 depicts five archetypes for securing the Canadian social or socio-economic union. The two approaches at the top of the "horseshoe"—unilateral federalism and EU-type confederalism are both "top-down" approaches. Unilateral federalism has been Canada's traditional post-war approach to the social union—a set of national principles or standards implemented via a federal system of transfers and overseen in a more or less unilateral way by the federal government. The EU confederal system is also top down in the sense that the standards are imposed on member states via a set of court-enforced "directives". However, the design of these directives is "bottom-up"—they are the result of member-state agreements. The remaining approaches in Chart 4 allow for varying degrees of sub-national input.

Chart 4: Five Archetypes for the Social Union

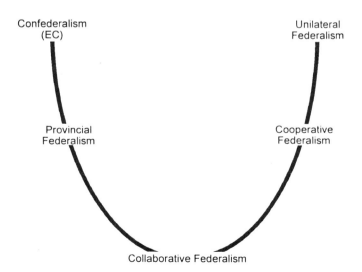

Confederalism
(EC)

Unilateral
Federalism

Provincial
Federalism

Cooperative
Federalism

Collaborative Federalism

Source: Margaret Biggs, *Building Blocks for Canada's New Social Union*, Working Paper No. F02, Canadian Policy Research Networks, June 1996.

Unilateral federalism has fallen on hard times. Part of the problem is that the increasing internationalization of the provincial economies, as reflected in the Table 1 data, implies that they desire and probably need greater manoeuverability in terms of redesigning their social policy infrastructures in their new competitive environments. Part, also, is due to the fact that Ottawa has misplayed its hand badly. The long series of unilateral freezes and caps and cuts to federal transfers has diminished Ottawa's moral authority and financial capacity to enforce these national principles. It was this emerging policy/instrument vacuum that led to my 1996 ACCESS model (*A Convention on the Canadian Economic and Social Systems*). ACCESS proposed two alternative models to unilateral federalism for addressing the internal social union. The first would probably fall in the "collaborative federalism" approach in terms of Chart 4—bringing in the provinces more fully and more formally into the design, implementation and monitoring of social Canada. The second was a largely interprovincial variant (falling under the "provincial federalism" archetype in terms of Chart 4), namely that the provinces would take the lead in developing conventions or accords, hopefully binding, to preserve and promote the economic union.

Even before the ACCESS model appeared on the scene, the provinces began to take up this challenge. Following upon the request in the 1995 federal budget that the provinces join with Ottawa to develop "mutual consent principles" to underpin the social union, the provinces (via the Ministerial Council on Social Policy Reform and Renewal) produced the impressive *Report To Premiers* which contained proposals along the lines of both ACCESS models. One tangible result of this process is the recent National Child Benefit, the initial proposal for which was contained in the *Report To Premiers*. And the even more recent "Calgary declaration" indicates that the premiers are continuing to play a much more important role in the operations of the federation than has heretofore been the case. The ACCESS-type models may not be the full answer, but Canada must surely devise some reasonable facsimile that challenges the provinces to shoulder enhanced "pan-Canadian" responsibilities commensurate with their increased powers.

Two final observations are in order. The first is that the emergence of Ontario as a region state heightens the need for some new intergovernmental machinery. And this is even more the case if Ontario opts for its own PIT collection system. The second is that, thus far at least, the "have" provinces appear to be in the forefront in terms of leadership on enhanced provincial participation in the overall governance of the federation. This is intriguing, given that these are the very provinces that, from a competitiveness and financial capacity perspective, probably have the most to gain from an erosion of national principles. Thus, there appears to be an appealing window of opportunity here that Ottawa might well want to capitalize on since in addition to securing the socio-economic union it will also make the governance of the federation more consistent with the emergence of economic region states.

D. LOOKING FORWARD

In drawing out the range of implications deriving from Ontario's new role we have limited ourselves largely to developments that are currently measurable or at least discernable. One can, of course, draw much more dramatic implications if the focus is forward looking. While our crystal-ball gazing is no better than that of our readers, we shall make a few comments toward this end.

It is already the case that if Ontario could not be the location of the next North America auto assembly plant, then the province would obviously prefer a Michigan location to a Vancouver location. This is what it means to be a region state! Looking to the future, one can envisage initiatives of the following nature:

- a move toward increased harmonization of the cross-border industrial/legal/ institutional frameworks;

- a move in the Baden-Würtemberg direction of signing agreements with other (cross-border) regions and/or entities;

- a move, probably on a sector by sector basis, to go beyond the FTA and NAFTA and to provide the Great Lakes equivalent of the single region for employment purposes created by Baden-Würtemberg, Alsace and Basel.

As written, all of these measures relate to industrial integration. However, at what point does this integration spill over to the social policy side? Ottawa's move to introduce a tax-on-base approach to the personal income tax may well serve to pre-empt a separate Ontario PIT, but these more flexible PIT arrangements will, nonetheless, pose challenges to the social union. One can easily imagine some provinces implementing a proportional tax structure while others may opt for a progressive tax structure. If and when policy areas such as welfare, training, tuition fees and even health become integrated with aspects of provincial income taxation (and here, Quebec with its own PIT is leading the way), preserving and promoting social Canada will increasingly require proactive provincial cooperation and coordination. Old style, top-down "negative integration" (e.g., thou shalt not impose residency requirements, thou shalt not impose user fees) will no longer suffice in the context of more integrated provincial subsystems in the social-policy/human-capital areas, especially since these subsystems will differ across provinces. This can be phrased differently: the ongoing provincial explosion in terms of creative initiatives and processes related to the design and delivery of social programs will likely result in a constellation of approaches to social Canada that will alter aspects of the Canadian social fabric to a degree that begins to mirror the manner in which globalization is altering the provincial economic environments. And this will be the case even if the existing pan-Canadian principles (e.g., the five Canada Health Act principles) remain in place. This serves to underscore the earlier message; namely that Canada needs new instruments in order to deal with the already altered geo-economy of the federation and the emerging diversity of the provincial social-policy subsystems. The ACCESS model may not be the solution, but some version of federal-provincial co-determination across a rather broad range of fronts seems inevitable if the federation is to preserve its east-west socio-economic union.

The typical counter to this is that further decentralization of the system will lead to the fragmentation of the socio-economic union. This may or may not be the case, but in any event it is largely irrelevant—decentralization is upon us, on both the economic and social fronts. The real challenge is how to accommodate this enhanced decentralization. In this context, models such as ACCESS should not be viewed as harbingers of further decentralization but rather as new governance instruments designed to harness the powerful decentralizing forces in ways that preserve and promote our long-standing goals in terms of east-west socio-economic integration.

Conclusion

How inevitable is the emergence of Ontario as a North American region state? Thus far, the analysis has not broached much, if any, uncertainty. In part this is because major aspects of the analysis appear irreversible, or largely so, such as the increasing north-south integration of Ontario. But in other areas, the trends are clearly not cast in stone. As the federal government acquires more fiscal flexibility, the potential exists for creative leadership and legislation that could serve to steer Ontario away from some of the tendencies alluded to in the above analysis. But the challenge for Ottawa is to exercise this newly acquired flexibility in full recognition of the interplay of the forces of globalization and the knowledge/information revolution on Ontario and the federation generally. Not to put too fine a point on this, Ottawa is not yet in this mindset. Reverting to the old-style Ottawa approach to federal-provincial fiscal relations is almost guaranteed to exacerbate the challenge.

Ontarians also have the potential for stemming aspects of this tide. We think it is fair to say that Harris and company are far more enamoured with Ontario's current policy thrust than are individual Ontarians. If the Conservatives deliver on their mandate and, in particular, if they balance the budget and (much less likely) if they meet their employment creation targets, Ontarians may well come on side. It seems to us that this would essentially make the emergence of an Ontario region state a fait accompli. However, writing in the midst of the controversial municipal/institutional revolution, it is anything but clear that the Harris government can successfully see these dual revolutions to a successful end. But even here, basic elements of the region state analysis will carry forward to any new Ontario administration.

Nonetheless, it is apparent that the Ontario that many of us have come to know and love (and, for some non-Ontarians, to hate) is no more. We may not know precisely where we are going but the pervasiveness of the economic forces means that we cannot go back: there is no status quo.

By default, as it were, this also means that we have to rethink and remake Canada and Canadian federalism. The vision we have been articulating is that, triggered by the emergence of Ontario as a North American region state, Canada as the world's largest developed federation must likewise evolve in a creative way. In our view the pervasiveness of economic forces necessarily means devolving greater autonomy to the regions so that they can pursue their distinctive economic futures. The major challenge to the operation of the federal system is to develop new and creative instruments to ensure that the new east-west railway—social policy—remains alive and well. This is a daunting challenge since there will be pressures from many quarters to unwind this east-west social policy and to have it follow the north-south trading system. Were this to occur, we citizens in the upper half of North America would become, in effect, northern Americans. This is among the foremost fears of the emergence of Ontario as a region state and, by extension, among the foremost challenges arising from the analysis in this paper. We must remain distinct, socially-economically. An important corollary is that it would be a mistake of the first order to link Ontario as a region state to the ascension to power of the Mike Harris Conservatives. While Harris has clearly and directly advanced the conception of Ontario as a North American region state, the underlying forces and pressures transcend Harris. The view that all would be right if only the Ontario Conservatives would somehow disappear is a dangerous illusion.

The reality is that Ontario's shift from heartland to economic region state is more or less inevitable and its implications strike at the very heart of Canadian federalism and, indeed, of Canada. In other words this is every bit as much a national challenge as it is an Ontario challenge, especially since similar pressures are driving BC and Quebec. If we can but grasp the new geo-economic realities, the opportunities for maintaining a distinct society in the upper half of North America in the millennium are eminently achievable. But if Laurier's vision of Canada is to extend to the twenty-first century, this will clearly call not so much for a renewed Canada as a renewal of the operations of Canadian federalism. But this has always been our strong suit. Setting aside the last decade or so when we became enamoured with constitutional solutions to what were, for the most part, political challenges, our history as a federation is replete with creative political, institutional and legislative responses to internal and external forces (Courchene 1995).

The time is once again at hand for us Ontarians and us Canadians to draw on our innate creativity to ensure that Canada again mirrors our collective aspirations from coast to coast to coast. But these aspirations must be consistent with the reality that Ontario is now a North American region state.

Notes

* This paper was written while I was completing *From Heartland to North America Region State: The Society, Fiscal and Federal Evolution of Ontario* (1998), (with Colin R. Telmer). Much of what appears below also appears, albeit in a different context, in the Courchene-Telmer book.

1. The sources for the information in Chart 1 and Table 1 are different. Hence the data tell a somewhat different quantitative story, but not a different qualitative story.

2. While Ontario has not as yet tipped its hand in terms of whether or not it will follow through on implementing its own PIT, there has been a fundamental shift in the nature of the shared personal income tax system. In December of 1997, Ottawa announced that, beginning in year 2000, the provinces will have the freedom to mount their own rate and bracket structures against the federally determined tax base. This represents a marked shift from the status quo, where provinces are limited to applying a single rate against federal tax owing. In the parlance of the PIT, this is a shift from "tax on tax" to "tax on base" or "tax on income". By way of implications, this represents a very significant further transfer of powers to the provinces, not only in terms of influencing overall income distribution but as well in creating flexibility for the provinces to use their portion of the PIT as a coordination and reconciliation instrument for designing integrated socio-economic subsystems. Moreover, this will presumably

complicate Ontario's decision with respect to its own PIT, since the new tax-on-base approach goes a considerable distance toward encompassing the potential advantages of a separate PIT.

References

Bell, Daniel (1987) "The World and the United States in 2013", *Daedalus*, 116:1-31.

Biggs, Margaret (1996) *Building Blocks for Canada's New Social Union*, Working Paper F02. Ottawa: Canadian Policy Research Networks.

Castells, Manuel (1996) *The Rise of the Network Society* (Cambridge: Blackwells).

Courchene, Thomas J. (1989) *What Does Ontario Want? The Coming of Age of Robarts' Confederation of Tomorrow Conference*. York University: Robarts Centre For Canadian Studies.

Courchene, Thomas J. (1995) *Celebrating Flexibility: An Interpretive Essay on the Evolution of Canadian Federalism*. The 1995 C.S. Howe Benefactors Lecture, Toronto: C.D. Howe Research Institute.

Courchene, Thomas J. (1996) *ACCESS: A Convention on the Canadian Economic and Social Systems*. Toronto: Ministry of Intergovernmental Affairs, Queen's University: The John Deutsch Institute for the Study of Economic Policy (forthcoming).

Courchene, Thomas J. (1997) "Globalization, Free Trade and Canadian Political Economy" in Raymond M. Hébert and Raymond Théberge (eds.) *Canada: Horizons 2000*. Winnipeg: Presses Universitaires de Saint-Boniface, 125-162.

Courchene, Thomas J. (1997a) "The PIT and the Pendulum: Reflections on Ontario's Proposal to Mount Its Own Personal Income Tax System", mimeo, Queen's University: School of Policy Studies.

Courchene, Thomas J. with Colin R. Telmer (1998) *From Heartland to North American Region State: The Social, Fiscal and Federal Evolution of Ontario*. Toronto: Faculty of Management, University of Toronto.

Crane, David (1997) "Trade Patterns Eroding Our Nation", *The Toronto Star* (January 5), F.2.

Drucker, Peter (1986) "The Changed World Economy", *Foreign Affairs* 64 (Spring), 1-17.

Hartt, Stanley H. (1992) "Sovereignty and the Economic Union" in Stanley H. Hartt et al (eds.) *Tangled Web: Legal Aspects of Deconfederation*. Toronto: C.D. Howe Institute, 3-31.

Helliwell, John (1996) "Do National Borders Matter for Quebec Trade", *Canadian Journal of Economics*

Helliwell, John and John McCallum (1995) "National Borders Still Matter for Trade", *Policy Options* 16 (July/August), 44-48.

Horsman, Mathew and Andrew Marshall (1994) *After the Nation State: Citizens, Tribalism and the New World Disorder*. London: Harper Collins.

Keating, Michael (1994) "The Political Economy of Regionalism", mimeo, London: Department of Political Science, University of Western Ontario.

Lecoq, Bruno (1991) "Organisation industrielle, organisation territoriale: une approche intégrée fondée sur le concept de réseau", *Revue d'Économie Régionale et Urbaine* 34:321-342.

McCallum, John (1995) "National Borders Matter: Canada-US Regional Trade Patterns", *American Economic Review* (June), 615-623.

Ministerial Council on Social Policy Renewal and Reform (1996) *A Report to Premiers* (This Report can be obtained from the intergovernmental secretariat of any province).

Newhouse, John (1997) "Europe's Rising Regionalism", *Foreign Affairs* 76 (January/February), 67-84.

Ohmae, Kenichi (1990) *The Borderless World.* New York: Harper Business.

Ohmae, Kenichi (1993) "The Rise of the Region State", *Foreign Affairs*, vol. 72, 78-87.

Ohmae, Kenichi (1995) *The End of the Nation State: The Rise of Region Economies* . New York: The Free Press.

Paquet, Gilles (1995) "Industrial Evolution in an Information Age" in Thomas J. Courchene (ed.) *Technology, Information and Public Policy*, Volume 3 of the Bell Canada Papers on Economic and Public Policy . Kingston: The John Deutsch Institute for the Study of Economic Policy, 197-230.

Reich, Robert (1991) *The Work of Nations.* New York: Alfred A. Knopf.

Savage, Premier John (1996) "The Two Canadas: The Devolution Debate", Address to Toronto's Empire Club (October 15).

Storper, Michael (1994) "The Resurgence of Regional Economics Ten Years Later", *European Urban and Regional Studies* vol. 2, No. 3 (191-221).

United Nations (1990) *Regional Economic Integration and Transnational Corporations in the 1990s: Europe 1992, North America and Developing Countries*, United Nations Center on Transnational Corporations, series A, no. 15. New York: United Nations.

Notes on Contributors
Notices biographiques des collaborateurs

Thomas J. Courchene, FRSC, is Director of the John Deutsch Institute for the Study of Economic Policy and is the Jarislowsky-Deutsch Professor of Economic and Financial Policy at Queen's University, Kingston. The author of over two hundred books and articles on Canadian policy issues, his research interests include financial deregulation, the political economy of Canadian federalism, and comparative federal systems.

Thomas J. Courchene, FRSC, est le directeur du John Deutsch Institute for the Study of Economic Policy et il occupe la chaire d'économie et de politique financière Jarislowsky-Deutsch à l'Université Queen's de Kingston. Auteur de plus de deux cents livres et articles sur des questions relatives aux politiques du Canada, il consacre ses travaux de recherche notamment à la déréglementation dans le secteur financier, à l'économie politique du fédéralisme canadien et à l'étude comparative des systèmes fédéraux.

Ursula M. Franklin, CC, FRSC, holds a Ph.D. in experimental physics and has taught at the University of Toronto for the past twenty years. As a member of the Department of Metallurgy and Materials Science, she has conducted research into the structure and properties of materials, both ancient and modern, as well as into the history and the social impact of technology.

Ursula M. Franklin, CC, FRSC, a un doctorat en physique expérimentale et enseigne depuis vingt ans à University of Toronto. Membre du corps professoral du Département de métallurgie et des sciences des matériaux, elle a conduit des travaux de recherche sur la structure et les propriétés des matériaux anciens et modernes ainsi que sur l'histoire et les incidences sociales de la technologie.

Dr. Henry Friesen, OC, FRSC, is President of the Medical Research Council of Canada and is an internationally renowned medical scientist, educator and endocrinologist. During his career, he has held numerous university positions as well as serving on national and international committees and task forces on medical research. He has received many honours for his research including the Gairdner Foundation Award and the Izaak Walton Killam Memorial Scholarship.

Le Dr. Henry Friesen, OC, FRSC, président du Conseil de recherches médicales du Canada, est un scientifique, un professeur et un endocrinologue de renommée internationale. Pendant son éminente carrière, il a occupé plusieurs charges universitaires et a fait partie de nombreux comités et groupes de travail nationaux et internationaux sur la recherche médicale. Ses travaux de recherche lui ont valu de multiples distinctions dont le prix de la Fondation Gairdner et la bourse commémorative Izaak Walton Killam.

Gisèle Painchaud est doyenne de la Faculté des sciences de l'éducation de l'Université de Montréal. Elle a fait des études en linguistique, en science politique et en éducation. Ses recherches portent sur le développement de la compétence en langue écrite (lecture et écriture), sur le curriculum en langues secondes et sur l'éducation des minorités. Elle est présentement présidente de l'Association francophone des doyens et directeurs d'éducation du Canada.

Gisèle Painchaud is Dean of the Faculty of Education at Université de Montréal. She holds degrees in linguistics, political science and education. She is widely published in the areas of school and workplace literacy, curriculum studies in second languages, and minority education. She is currently president of the Association francophone des doyens et directeurs d'éducation du Canada.

Gilles Paquet, CM, MSRC, is the Director of the Centre on Governance at the University of Ottawa. In addition to holding various university positions, he has been president of many Canadian associations. He has authored / co-authored or edited some 20 books and written over 250 papers or chapters in books on issues ranging from economic history of Canada, to urban, regional, and industrial development, trade and technology, regulation of socio-economic systems, public management and governance.

Gilles Paquet, CM, MSRC, est le directeur du Centre d'études sur la gouvernance de l'Université d'Ottawa. En plus d'occuper plusieurs charges universitaires, il a été le président de nombreuses associations canadiennes. Il a écrit ou édité une vingtaine d'ouvrages et plus de 250 articles de revue ou chapitres dans des ouvrages sur des sujets qui vont de l'histoire économique du Canada au management public et à la gouvernance en passant par les études urbaines et régionales, l'organisation industrielle, et la régulation des systèmes socio-économiques.

David F. Robitaille is Professor of Mathematics Education and head of the Department of Curriculum Studies at the University of British Columbia. He is the International Coordinator of the Third International Mathematics and Science Study, a major study of the teaching and learning of mathematics and science at the elementary and secondary school levels. Professor Robitaille is the author of more than one hundred scholarly papers as well as an author of mathematics textbooks for elementary and secondary schools.

David F. Robitaille est professeur de didactiques des mathématiques et directeur de la Faculté d'éducation à University of British Columbia. Il est le coordonnateur international de la Troisième enquête internationale sur les mathématiques et les sciences, un vaste projet de recherche sur l'enseignement et l'apprentissage des mathématiques et des sciences aux niveaux primaire et secondaire. Le professeur Robitaille est l'auteur de plus de cent communications savantes et de plusieurs manuels de mathématiques pour les classes primaires et secondaires.

Duncan G. Sinclair was appointed Chair of Ontario's Health Services Restructuring Commission in the early spring of 1996. A long-time resident of Kingston, Dr. Sinclair retired in June as Vice-Principal for Health

Sciences and Dean of the Faculty of Medicine of Queen's University. Dr. Sinclair has served on a number of boards and advisory bodies including the Public Hospitals Act Steering Committee, the Provincial Cancer Network, and the Premier's Council on Health, Well-Being, and Social Justice. He was also a member of the National Forum on Health.

Duncan G. Sinclair a été nommé président de la Commission de restructuration des services de santé de l'Ontario au début du printemps 1996. Résident de longue date de Kingston, le Dr. Sinclair a fait valoir en juin ses droits à la retraite alors qu'il était vice-recteur des sciences de la santé et doyen de la Faculté de médecine de l'Université Queen's. Il a siégé à de nombreux conseils et offices consultatifs dont le Comité directeur de la Loi sur les hôpitaux publics, le Réseau provincial du cancer et le Conseil du Premier ministre sur la santé, le bien-être et la justice sociale. Il a également été membre du Forum national sur la santé.